IT'S OK NOT TO BE OK

ARRAM KONG

It's OK NOT to be OK

www.arramkong.co.uk

1st Edition July 2006

ISBN 10: 0-9552862-0-4
ISBN 13: 978-0-9552862-0-9

Printed and bound by Antony Rowe Ltd, Eastbourne

A Kong Publishing
2 Corringham Road
Wembley Middlesex, HA9 9QA, England

CAUTION

The techniques and advice given in this Self Help book are not intended to replace medical or psychiatric treatment.

Readers with medical or psychiatric conditions should consult with their appropriate health practitioner before putting these ideas into practice for themselves or others.

Acknowledgments

I would like to thank Gayatri Raj, my ex- client and dear friend, for nagging me persistently over the last few years to get this material out in book form. I met Gayatri in June of 2003. She was recommended to seek my counsel by a mutual friend of ours. In the various meetings that we had in 2003, I introduced and shared with Gayatri my concepts on Energy Medicine and this intrigued her. She is a graduate of a scientific background and my teachings contradicted her "programming". Nevertheless, she was open minded enough to try it out and discovered how very beneficial it was for her.

Over the years and months on occasions when we would meet, Gayatri suggested I write a book on what I had shared with her as she thought people would benefit from my experience. I told her that I didn't even know where to begin. She suggested that I just write down what I shared with my clients. I commented that this would take too long and decided not to take the matter further.

It's funny, but when you are really meant to do something it never goes away. Gayatri was like a Jack-in-the-box that kept popping up and saying, "When are you going to write your book?" Every time I closed the lid, she would pop up again!

After years of her continuous pestering I finally succumbed to her request. I told her that I would attempt to write the book provided she personally read the chapters I wrote and help me with feedback. She agreed and in June 2005 I started the book and have just finished it in April 2006. She has been a constant help and I can only say that without her help this material would not be available.

I would also like to thank all the hundreds of clients I worked with. Their progress and faith in my technique has helped themselves heal and encouraged me. The information and feedback through their successful treatments are part of the material in this book.

However, my biggest source of teachers has been family members, ex wife, ex girlfriends, colleagues and friends; it is only in hindsight after the event that I became aware that they were my teachers. My dear father who is very controlling, manipulative, inflexible and extremely unforgiving gave me the best opportunity to learn about letting go, being flexible and forgiveness. My loving mother can 'never' resist a bargain, and being very predetermined in her ways allowed me to learn about being satisfied with what I have and to be patient. Angelika, my ex wife, a very cautious lady and planner of the future, allowed me to learn about being fearless and living in the present. My sister Angelene's gift to me was how to be unconditionally generous with others. Bashi Luxton, my very dear friend, allowed me to understand truly what empathy and compassion were about. Josie, my partner, has taught me about patience and unconditional consistency. My late brother Augustine and Samantha my second eldest daughter have taught me about minding my own business and allowing people to get on with their lives irrespective of my opinions. My younger children have been my greatest teachers especially Jonathan, my son, and runner up his sister, Laura. Whilst I thought that they were constantly a pain in the butt when they were growing up, they only reflected back to me what I needed to heal within myself. They have taught me about non-judgement, self-acceptance, unconditional love and ***" It's OK NOT to be OK."***

Table of Contents

How Do You Eat An Elephant?

"Go as far as you can see and when you get there you will always be able to see further." Zig Ziglar

At first, the thought of writing a book on self-help was daunting, especially because I had never been a writer or done anything quite like this before. I remembered that at school, English wasn't my favourite subject and upon starting this book I asked myself, " Where do I start?" The phrase that came to me was "How do you eat an elephant?..........One bite at a time".

Often when we are worried, or we are confused, our minds will become carried away thinking about all the problems, scenarios...etc., which we might face. This in turn leads to us worry more and even panic. Now, every time I am confronted with a situation that needs a quick fix, or an immediately answer, I ask myself this question, "How do you eat an elephant?" It stops me in my track of expectancy, brings my awareness to the present time and stops me thinking unconsciously for a while. I stop guessing about the future and over reflecting on the past. Almost instantly I calm down as I realise my situation and my mind becomes open to possibilities, or at least the situation does not seem so bad. My situation becomes more manageable and I don't go into a stressful or panic mode. I am going to share with you various techniques that will help you to realise your situation better and to help you achieve calmness in your mind.

I began this book by writing a little each time I sat down and I found that a sentence became a paragraph, a paragraph became a page and then more pages. I bit my elephant one piece at a time, which confirmed my belief that everything starts from small beginnings and grows. Life is also something like this. Life is never the same; it is always changing, even a little at a time. My observation taught me that ***THERE WILL ALWAYS BE CHANGE IN EVERYTHING.***

It is important to understand that things evolve and there is no point wasting time and energy over worrying and over planning things. As I wrote this book, I allowed the contents to evolve and in this way stopped myself from wasting time and personal energy thinking about how this book should be or could be or must be. Do not waste your energy judging and thinking about what I am going to tell you, just read "one piece of the elephant at a time."

MY BEGINNING

I want to tell you about my personal journey, not about my 63 years but share with you some of the major changes that I have experienced in my life. Perhaps this will help you to shift your perceptions of life and place you in a better space both mentally and physically. After all, ***the reason you are reading this book is that you are searching for answers for your current situation.*** You are hoping that there is something in this book that may help you. I am going to share with you some of my observations as a teacher, healer, student and patient. I am neither a scientist nor a doctor, but what I will share with you is a result of my research into alternative healing therapies and many years studying and understanding ***energy medicine.*** I feel confident that you will find some of what I share with you will make perfect sense, but perhaps other points will require you to keep an open mind. Please, keep an open mind and read this book to its end.

During the past years as a therapist, healer, patient, student, parent and lover I have learnt how the body heals. By being open-minded, setting no limits on myself, remembering "how to eat an elephant" and accepting that there is always change I have arrived at my temporary destiny. My present moment is only a part of my life's journey and it will not be the end for me. There are many more changes for me to experience, as remember I said life evolves. ***What you are experiencing today is only your present destiny.***

For now I need to recap and share with you what I have discovered and hope that you will benefit from my experiences. My life didn't change overnight. It was changing all the time but I wasn't aware of it as it was so subtle. The same can be said for your life, it has always been changing but your pre-occupations to create and live a life according to your expectations, or of those around you, has left you short-sighted and unable to see this change.

To realise my changes ***the Universe*** (for those who do not believe in God, or some greater power) sent me a "shock". I was stripped of my wealth! When I lost my fortune and then my family, I began to look at life differently. Previously, money had played an important part in my life and in the past I had been so successful at making money I was able to retire at 45 years old. To me, money was everything. Money was first and everything else came second. My beliefs were that if I had money I could make everything all right. I could make others happy, could buy happiness and find or buy love for my family. For me, ***Money made my world go round. However, since then I have learnt that money really is the root of many of our pains. I wish you to understand that you need money to live but that it does not need to control you. Do not give away your powers to it the way I did.***

I didn't like my misfortunes. They took me out of my comfort zone (current lifestyle) and so I played the victim. I didn't like change and didn't want to take responsibility for what was happening to me, so I looked to blame someone. Sound familiar?

Well, in actual fact, the traumatic experience was very lucky for me as it allowed me to change/grow into the person I am today. In retrospect I feel I was let off lightly and spared the pains of a wake up call in the form of losing a love one, or facing a life threatening illness. All I lost was my wealth and my status.

The whole experience has made me a more caring, loveable, and compassionate person. I unconditionally accept myself and others, with love growing every day. I certainly judge others less now and allow people to be who they are. I no longer have expectations of how they should behave and wish them to be who I want them to be. ***I have become more acceptable of "what is", and aware of my thoughts***. You can say I am more conscious now.

This new "me" compared to the one before my disaster is totally different, like an alien. During my transition my family and close friends thought I had lost it, "He's gone mad," they said. I had changed so much that they found it difficult to accept the new me, as they wanted me to be the way I was. They did not want/like change; they wanted me to be the same as they had always known me in the past. The majority of us have been taught and conditioned to think and accept that **CHANGE is SCARY**. This is totally not true. ***Change is inevitable, there is only change, and when we begin to understand this we will start to heal our past. Do not be scared of yourself or loved ones changing.***

My change began by me seeking answers to life, ways to heal my physical and emotional pains and wanting to find out what life was all about. It certainly wasn't about making lots of money as I had been there, worn the T-shirt, and didn't experience real happiness. I didn't know who I was and I suppose you could say that I woke up one morning to start my spiritual journey. I attended many self- help courses and read hundreds of books on different modalities of healing and how others perceived life. I became an avid student of life.

I have come to the conclusion that one of the most powerful ways to heal is through LOVE of the SELF and through conserving our ENERGIES. With the help of others and my observations, I have been able to help hundreds of people over the past years acquire a better quality of life. So now I am guided to write this book and hopefully share my knowledge with the many thousands out there who seek help.

Your Beginning

"You can have anything you want if you will give up the belief that you can't have it." Obvious

To start with, I first need you to understand that to begin healing i.e. to change, YOU have to be honest with yourself and say that, "I am not happy, that I am dissatisfied with who I am and/or my situation." If you are happy then there is no need to be reading this material as you are content with your life at this very moment.

However, if we are honest, then in reality the majority of us are unhappy, which is why there is so much misery, discontentment, disease and sickness in our world. The majority of us are always complaining that we are victims, or wish our lives away, or wish that we were in different situations. For example, we wish to live in another country, to be in a partnership, to have different parents....etc,...etc. We sing a song "Why can't I be happy ...if only...IF (such a thing could change in my life)......my life would be better.... IF....(*you fill in the blank. I suggest that you keep a journal whilst you read my book and put the list in your journal*).....I would be happy", ...the list of IF's is endless.

Have you ever wondered how you became like this? How you became conditioned to be dissatisfied with life? Who taught you this "song"? Have you ever noticed how dissatisfied people around you are today? Do you know how you became the dissatisfied person you are today?

Let me start by sharing with you what influences our life most besides our parents, partners, teachers, siblings, friends and enemies. I want you to cast your mind back to your childhood and remember how many times you were left alone to watch TV or to entertain yourselves. For those of you who, as a child, were never left in front of a TV, you were spared. I want to talk to the majority of us who have been watching TV since we were children and have now as adults become addicted to it.

Have you ever noticed what is being advertised on TV? Go and list what is being advertised in your journal, and if you cannot recall, then I suggest that over the next few days when you are watching the TV you make a list of the things you see advertised. Also, notice what is advertised in the newspapers and/or magazines that you read. We will start from here in order to understand what is really influencing us on a daily basis. After all, you must recognise that if advertising was ineffective, advertisers would not spend billions of dollars trying to get their messages across to us. And yes, we are definitely receiving their messages.

This is the beginning of your self-awareness journey. Are you ready? So, what influences us on a daily basis? We are constantly bombarded with messages telling us that we LACK something in our lives. Either we do not have enough money, we need a holiday, a new car… or the messages go on to tell us how we should look, what to eat, what to take when we are ill. The recurrent message we receive is loud and clear……. We are lacking!

WE ARE TOLD ON A DAILY BASIS THAT WE ARE NOT GOOD ENOUGH AND WE ARE NOT ABLE TO THINK FOR OURSELVES.

Having seen the daily adverts we are bombarded with, are you then surprised that we believe we are lacking something in our lives? Looking at children's programmes today, is it any wonder that parents are placed under immense pressure to provide their child with the latest gismo? Children receive a message that to be "in" they need to have "X". Having such an item will confirm they "belong" to the right group, they will be accepted by others and they must be cool! They see a message that they are "not good enough" but that designer clothes, shoes, toys or even eating a particular type of food will make them acceptable.

Remember that this "bombardment" is going on a globally scale and as we, the child, grow older it becomes part of our lives that we do not feel good enough. We become totally dependent on external things/influences to make us happy, satisfied, content, or whole. There is another message we receive daily, have a look at the news-papers, listen to the radio or watch TV and notice it. The majority of the news is about FEAR. ***So with daily dosages of "FEAR and LACK of…" it is of no surprise that today there are many stressed and sick people in our society.***

Our daily medicine is - we are not good enough, we need more, there is something lacking in our lives and to be careful out there as there is always danger lurking around. This "medicine" is provided by the TV, newspapers, and of course the gossip we pay attention to. News informs us of how dangerous life is, how much we are lacking and that we are not satisfied with what we have, we should have more and more. Hence, what do we talk about? We wish that our lives would or could be different-BUT WHY?

For those of you who do not suffer from "a lack of", and are not afraid, you are lucky. You have been spared these experiences or maybe you have understood these to be only illusions created by a greedy society. You probably believe in yourself more and love yourself more and more each day. Good on you! Keep up the good work and now help others who are stuck thinking that they do not have enough. Keep telling yourself that "I am in control" and "I have a choice". Those who have not reached this point are weak and not in control, dependent on someone or something to tell them how to live. Remember that such insight does not mean you are better than anyone else but that you are lucky to have a greater awareness and to have been shown "The Way". ***Everyone has the same opportunity of getting out of his or her situation.***

If we wish to change or to realise that we are being presented with an unrealistic reality, we need to accept that we have been conditioned. Now this is hard for us to understand as we think that everybody else thinks like us. Wrong, each and everyone thinks differently. The reason I am saying this is because of how we think others will think of us. This is only our judgement of ourselves and we think others think of us in the same way, as we assume that they are thinking like us to have that assumption.

Let me take you back to the beginning of your journey (your life). ***When you were born you were pure love, with no corruptions or dysfunctional behaviour.*** Just like a brand new computer with no programmes. You had the capability of doing everything and nothing at the same time. However, your "programming" depended on your programmers and who do you think your programmers were? Your parents or whoever brought you up. You started life as a baby/child taking on their beliefs. Most parents will unknowingly bring up their child the way they were, or treat their child as they were, or make great efforts to bring up the child the way they wanted to be raised. Hence, you have taken on your "programmer's" characteristics becoming like them. This is not to say that your upbringing was good or bad; it is just a fact that I wish you to understand. Your programmers brought you up the only way they knew and could not do differently because they didn't know how to.

Guess what? You will do the same with your children, passing on your parent's beliefs unless a day comes on your journey when you decide to change. At a point in your life, you may realise that the life you have is not the one you want, and you become aware that it **"is"** possible for you to lead the life you want. You do not have to take what is being offered. However, such awareness usually occurs after you have had a painful experience in your life's journey. For example: loss of a loved one, a broken relationship, being betrayed, loss of fortune/job, being seriously ill, or loss of something very valuable in your life. This great and fortunate (you will say terrible and unfortunate) event causes you to change. Please note that if this "event" has not happened to you yet, it will. It will be your wake up call. It is your choice as to whether you wish to take notice of it. ***Pain is an indication for us to change. Pain forewarns us that something is wrong and we need to take notice.***

Getting To Know A Little Of You

"Your medicine is in you, and you do not observe it. Your ailment is from yourself, and you do not register it." Hazrat Ali

The majority of us do not know who we are and what our patterns are. I like to change the word patterns to addictions. We have an addiction to everything that is in our reality, some we like and some we dislike. Those that we like we will do more of and those that we dislike we avoid. Each individual has his or her own likes and dislikes. The ones we like give us pleasure and the ones we dislike give us pain. Most of us tend to bend toward pleasure and avoid pain. The more we repeat something the more it is in control of us, and eventually we are controlled by that behaviour/pattern. We become addicted to that emotion. Yes, you need to accept that you have given your power to your patterns/addictions. We are not in control. Let me expand on this further so that you may begin to understand what I am talking about.

As you begin to grow older you learn through trial and error. You do the things that give you the most pleasure and avoid those that give you pain or do less of such activities. Hence your identity and behaviour are created on pain and pleasure. You started to make sense of your world by noticing what works for you and what does not. You created your boundaries/understanding through pain and pleasure. I suggest that you make your list of your experiences of your pain and pleasure now in your journal.

The people that brought you up also set your boundaries through pain and pleasure. Therefore you have unknowingly become limited, as you have never been allowed to expand and express yourself limitlessly. You weren't allowed to and so, you do not know any better, and have assumed that this is how life is. Again, your boundaries were associated with pain and pleasure and so if you dared to go against your parents, peers, siblings, your culture, your religion, your teachers, your environment, you were punished or made to fear punishment. Hence, from a very young age, you have been taught to and conditioned to conform.

By conforming, and doing what others wanted us to do, we have been controlled via their beliefs. We adopted their behaviour and since we didn't know any better this is how we have grown up. Remember there is no right or wrong way of being brought up. What I am trying to get across to you is a greater understanding of your background. There is really nothing wrong with you, only that you have been conditioned from a very young age and moulded to be the person that you are today. ***The good news is you can change if you are unhappy with the way you are.***

THE CONFORMIST

During your early childhood, if you were an obedient child and conformed to your early carers' requests (in most cases our parents), and what you did happened to give you pleasure; you would keep repeating the request whenever presented with the opportunity. This obedience would be linked to treats (sweets, toys, food, a hug, a compliment, kindness) and you liked this feeling of pleasure. Unknowingly, you were being controlled to behave in this manner to receive a reward. This became part of your strategy and pattern for growing up, becoming addicted to the pleasurable feelings and behaviour.

Your strategy has been "If I please someone, I will be rewarded" so you have always tried to please and wanted to be liked/loved and rewarded. Those times when we didn't want to do what was requested of us, and instead do more interesting things, we were punished and told that "you are bad, naughty". Hence, "pleasing" became your way of life, choosing to put others first. This childhood taught you that ***if you dared to put yourself first, you were selfish.*** Are you getting my drift?

In the main, we have become a society of conformists and we have totally given our powers away to others. Some of you may be thinking, "hold on, I am not like that I am the opposite of what you are saying, I am a non-conformist, I am a rebel", please wait. I will come to you after I have explained to the conformist why they are who they are, and then explain to the non-conformist why they are different. Patience please!

Those of you who are Conformists; you were programmed to give your power away at an early age. By power I mean ***you allowed others to control you***. Is it any wonder that we find it so difficult to think for ourselves? And why we are so easily led? The good news is that you can do something about it NOW. You became their slaves unknowingly as you didn't know any better. The point is the people that brought you up and installed those disciplines also didn't know any better! Monkey sees monkey do and the majority of us have become a society of followers.

Our teachers (I use this term loosely as I believe that everyone in our lives is our teacher and we can learn from them) were only doing what was done to them when they were young and they didn't know any better. We learn to conform and if we dared go against them, we were punished. If we dared speak up, we were outlawed and through fear of pain we conform and didn't dare speak up. If we repeated this pattern of being outspoken, we were again punished and if we carried on and still didn't conform, we were outcaste from society. Again you can see how FEAR was instilled in us at a very early age. So we adopted our teachers' beliefs and these became part of our way of living.

We live in fear and look to others to approve us to make us feel good. We please others to fulfil our identity and think that this is how it should be. (Their liking us, approving of us means that we are loved) Isn't this sad?

Never mind, this section is only about increasing your awareness of your background; you can change and become fearless by learning to love yourself, not by pleasing others but by pleasing yourself. It is possible that some of you are saying "but I like helping others, I have joy from it, and I am not fearful and I do love myself." If that is the case, then you are one of the lucky ones and you do not need to read any further. However, before you leave me let me ask you one question. Are you content with where you are now in your life today and are you in good health? If you are, then you do not need any help, but if you are not sure and are ill or tired most of the time then hang in there and all will be revealed to you. I wish to talk to those of you who want/need help and I am trying to show you how you have become the person you are today.

Recap:

FEAR from a very early age has been induced into you and you have learnt to conform, otherwise you were punished. Those of you who think differently understand at least this that all you are today has been a learnt behaviour pattern from your early childhood. Everything that you are today is learnt, or copied into your current behaviour. This behaviour has become your identity, the EGO. You are the sum total of all your life experiences and that is all you. ***You are all your conditioning and addictions.***

WHO ARE THE NON-CONFORMISTS?.... THE REBEL

Going back to the beginning of our journey, when we were young and conformed we would be rewarded by being liked, showered with affection/attention, given sweets, toys, foods, etc. (rewards). Hence, we would carry on conforming in order to be rewarded as this made us feel good. We became the Pleaser. The "love" as we understood it was CONDITIONAL. However, some of us would conform and not receive any attention as we were EXPECTED to behave in a certain way having been shown the behaviour once or twice.

In this instance, when we became pleasers, and received nothing, we would think "what's the point of pleasing, I am not being rewarded." What do you think happens to the child that grows up with this thought? Such children usually come from families where the parents are too busy with their lives, or there are too many children and the parents do not have the time to meet the demands of all of them. Alternatively, the parents might not be well, being sickly, dysfunctional, addicts do not have the energy to look after themselves or their children. Perhaps a lone parent who does not get enough support. With some families there is a great expectancy from their lives and that of their children, so they work hard but neglect their children's and their own personal needs. They believe that in the end the sacrifice justifies the means.

Those of us who didn't receive any/little attention over a period of time learnt that if we did something different, perhaps someone might pay attention to us. So we became rebels. We misbehaved and didn't conform. Yes, we were noticed but we would now receive the wrong type of reward/ attention, being punished instead. We were scolded, shouted at, or even beaten. In these instances even the wrong type of attention is better than no attention at all. In some cases after being punished the person punishing us might have felt guilty for perhaps being too hasty and so, feeling sorry, they would then treat us (the child) with kindness. This might have been by way of kind words, cuddles or the giving of sweets, presents or treats. Now, this will really confuse the child. "When I conform I don't get noticed, when I don't conform I get shouted at or punished and then I get rewarded, and I am being noticed." Remember that we learn through trial and error, and in this particular case we have a person that will grow up being a non-conformist because this is the way their beliefs have been set up.

There is another type of non-conformist. There are those of us who, when growing up, weren't noticed at all and by taking on rebel characteristics we only received punishments and no rewards. Such a person grows up to be angry, likely to be always in trouble and hence is labelled a "trouble-maker" by society. It is not the person who is bad and deserves a punishment; it is just the way they know how to get attention.

Being good, conforming, brought NO attention so such individuals amongst us try the opposite to see what happens. Most are not aware of how they behave, only seeing (at an unconscious level) that being in trouble is a way of getting attention even if it is not rewarded correctly. They associate some sort of attention as being liked because they have been noticed. In fact, all they wanted is to be noticed and an acknowledgement of their existence. These are the children who create havoc at home, at school and drive their parents/guardian crazy. If only we were trained to know that when a child is naughty all they want is some attention, to be noticed and it will make all our lives easier.

What I am trying to get across to you is how at an early age ***our beliefs were set up by others*** and through our own creative experiences in our early life. I know that this is a very large subject to tackle and there are literally hundreds of books that have been written about it, but I am trying to make it simplistic. I wish you to understand how you have been programmed and have become the person you are today. Again, let me repeat, this knowledge does not label us good or bad individuals, but gives us an awareness of who we are. By understanding how we have become "programmed" we no longer need to blame life or our parents, teachers… etc. We can release ourselves from being STUCK in old ways. We can begin to take responsibility for our lives by healing our past. This should excite you! This knowledge gives you the chance to re-program yourself, make changes, and look forward to leading a beneficial and fruitful life in the near future. We do not have to be a victim of our circumstances!

THE SPOILT BRATS

This is a breed of children who were allowed to do whatever they wanted. Probably their parents allowed the child to take control in order for them to have peace and quiet. They could not stand the nagging and the crying because all they wanted was a quiet time. However, by allowing the child to do what they wanted the parents have allowed their lives to be taken over. This is the start of a bully, the control freak child who only wants things their way and if they do not get it, they throw a tantrum. They must always win. When you start to punish such a child and try to reason with them, it is often already too late, as they will only scream more and drive you mad, leading to you giving in as you have always done in the past. In this situation the parent ends up pleasing the child and the child controls the situation and family. It becomes a constant battle with the child winning and having its way. We learn through trial and error, through pain and pleasure. As already explained there are many differences between what pain and pleasure do and lead to different outcomes as already highlighted in the earlier paragraphs.

Spoil brats tend to get their own way most of the time and end up being in control of most situations. Again, I want to stress that these children are not bad or that when they grow up they will be bad people, it is just the way they are.

Remember, as you read this book do not make judgements about the characters and traits mentioned. Do not go around analysing and labelling people to see which "type" of upbringing they have had. You should only observe the different types that are presented and attempt to identity yourself. It should only be that through acknowledging that different types of people exist, you begin to understand their background and have an understanding of their needs. ***I will not repeat this caution again about this in later*** *(chapters)*. Remember you are to just observe on how you have become who you are NOW.

THE PERFECTIONIST

Why do you think that some of us are perfectionists? Where have we learnt this trait? Again if we look at the early part of such an individual's journey, you will find they were programmed to be a perfectionist by their "keepers". They were criticized, judged, coaxed, punished, loved, abused, emotional blackmailed to be who they are today. When a parent/guardian constantly tells a child they could do better, the child grows up believing they are not good enough and must do better all the time. These children grow up to be high achievers but often are never really happy. They are preoccupied all the time, disappointed because of their own and/or others expectancy to do things better.

Sometimes, these individuals are capable high achievers who have become dropouts (rebels) because they do not like being pushed. They become very stubborn and will work at their own pace, with some becoming very disruptive. They end up drifting from career to career. Nevertheless, when they do find something that holds their interest they excel at it.

I am not going to expand any further on the subject of your character, traits and behaviour patterns, as I will just be duplicating the hundreds of books already written by professional people. My purpose is to inform you in a very simplistic way, and in a language that you can understand, that from a very young age (from birth) we have become conditioned to be who we are today.

Through trial and error, and with the help of our carers, we have moulded ourselves to be the person we are today.

MAKING SENSE OF IT ALL

I explained earlier to you how from a very young age we were programmed to become conformist or non-conformist. Hence, our experiences from childhood to adulthood have lead us to becoming pleasers or rebels, extroverts or introverts, givers or takers, spenders or misers, risk takers or cautious, argumentative or passive, confident or not confident, strong or weak, disciplined or undisciplined, tidy or untidy, ambitious or not ambitious, caring or uncaring, selfish or unselfish, optimistic or pessimistic. This list could be very long and I will leave you to fill in the ones that you think are associated with you and that I have missed out.

I just want you to be aware of some of your patterns. Take the opportunity to look at yourself consciously and decide where you are in the above examples. Take a pencil and circle the patterns that you think are you. You will probably find that you are a combination of many of the above mentioned. If I have missed your traits, just add them to the list for your reference; the list is only for your eyes. In fact you may find that you flip through the law of opposites, between the conformist and non-conformists. We fluctuate between the two depending on our teachers at the time.

Pain and Pleasure shape who we are today. Most of us lean towards pleasure and away from pain, leading to us spending much of our time undertaking "pleasurable" activities. We become addicted to pleasure in our attempts to avoid pain. But you need to understand that to understand what pleasure is we need to experience pain.

Have you wondered how people in abusive relationships can be treated so badly yet still not leave a relationship where they have been abused so badly? It is because the abused individual does not know any better; in their world there are no differences between pleasure and pain. From a very young age pleasure wasn't an option and they have never experienced it. They only know PAIN. These people come from abusive backgrounds, usually their parents were abused and perform such acts as they didn't know any better and so the pattern/behaviour is passed on.

Recap:

I have explained that your daily dosage by the media is of "Lack and Fear." I have shown you that when you were born you were programmed to be either a conformist or non-conformist. This I hope has allowed you to be more aware of yourself and understand why you behave the way you do today. It is likely that you have come to a realisation that you are unhappy with your situation, or maybe you are ill and are now looking for alternative ways to find hope. You may want to understand your purpose in life or reasons as to why you were born into this situation. Why are you unhappy? Why are you a VICTIM? Life at the moment is so cruel.

Remember, "How do you eat an elephant?"

Remedy: I would suggest that over the next 21 days you refrain from reading newspapers or watching the news or advertisements on TV. If you need to watch TV or read the papers, I suggest you try to be very selective at what you read or watch. I personally have not read the newspapers for years and seldom listen to the news or watch it on TV. Of course, I watch TV as there are many interesting documentary programmes and good films being shown. When it comes to the ads or news I will tend to ignore them or otherwise watch them with no attachment, observing only without being influenced.

Some have said to me that I am uneducated and unworldly due to my poor knowledge of current affairs and what is happening in the world. The truth of the matter is that it does not matter what is happening in the world as I cannot change it. But watching such things is likely to cause me to worry and lose my energy. Worry is a lost cause because it changes nothing. **STOP Worrying.**

We are First Energy Beings Rather Than Humans

"The Highest form of Ignorance is to reject something you know nothing about." Dr. Wayne Dyer

You are a whirling energy field! You may be surprised by this knowledge but the Ancients knew about the energy systems connected within the body many thousands of years ago. However, today very little is known about the connections between the seen and unseen worlds. By "seen" the physical world is implied and "unseen" the electrical, magnetic and energetic worlds. I would also add human emotions to the unseen worlds and I will cover this topic later on.

It has only been in the last century that people have become more aware of the unseen worlds. Historically, most methods of healing have been through the seen world, i.e. through physical aspects. We treat the symptoms that we can see and physically feel. Those that are unseen are considered as pure speculations.

There are some of you that are able to see the unseen world of fields. You will see different colours around a person or an object as you read their "Aura". The Aura comes from within the body and extents outwards about two feet. Imagine yourself within an egg and if you stood with your legs about one metre apart and stretched your hands out beside you, your aura is the oval shape around you. The different colours in your aura represent different emotions and states of health, which to a trained healer, informs them of your physical state of health. Through Kirlein Photography you can also see these fields. (This technique was invented by a Russian scientist and named after him). If you happen to visit a new age exhibition like the Mind, Body & Spirit held at Alexandra Palace in London every year, you can have a picture of your aura taken. Trained readers at the stands are able to give you an interpretation of the colours that surround your physical body in the photograph. The aura captured in the photo is an indication of your health at the time.

Some trained healers are also able to access your energy field by feeling your auric field (your energy field around your body) with their hands. Some individuals can even hear this energy as energy produces sound as well. It has a very high pitch tone and variations in the pitch represent different energy fields in your body. The "hearer" is able to listen to the pitches and interpret them. There are even some individuals who I refer to as "feelers". They have the skill to feel the different density of the energy that surrounds you and they will use this to interpret your current state of health. Now, the ignorant and untrained observer will say that all of this is nonsense and there is no energy field around us. However, I will remind you it is the conditioning from an early childhood that is making them refuse to accept this knowledge. They know only how to conform to the beliefs of their programmers.

All of us can access the reality and existence of this energy once we have been taught "how to". In actual fact, as children we were naturally able to see these colours but because the grown-ups of our society were ignorant of the existence of such energy fields we have not been encouraged to venture into this unseen world. Instead we were misinformed and told that we were imagining things. In reality, as children we were able to see different colours floating in the air like little round balloons or blobs of different sizes, from very minute to very large. We were able to see these blobs around people, objects or just floating in space. However, unfortunately, when we tried to tell our guardians about what we could see, we would be ignored. In fact, if we persisted to describe what we saw, we would be punished for being a "liar" and so we learnt to ignore what we saw. It is through not believing what we could see that we have become desensitised and unaware that such energy exists. Our unseen reality shifted to be only the physical reality.

Remember this book has been written in a simplistic manner. I want to give you a basic understanding on how energy works in your body and how you could prevent yourself from becoming ***dis-eased***.

The ancient Indians healed through the Chakra systems. Basic teachings of the chakra are that there are 7 energy centres in the body and the centres are all connected to all the different organs of the body. Imbalances or blockages of these chakras leads to the body being "dis-eased". Hence, a healer performed healing by passing energy through their hands to the different centres of the chakra in the body. This is how hands on healing developed.

The Ancients Chinese on the other hand healed with needles on the Meridians (Acupuncture points). There are some 366 points all over the body and they all connect to different organs of the body and to each other. If any part of the body's organ was dis-eased, needles were put into the points on the body that represented the organs path. The needles would clear the energy blockage, allowing the sick organs to physically heal. Scientists are beginning to discover the energy fields that surround the body through the study of Quantum Physics, after all, the body is made up of atoms, neutrons and electrons. However, such findings are struggling to be accepted in the traditional medical world.

Energy Follows Thoughts

"Energy is all there is." Albert Einstein

From this moment onwards it is very important that you have an open mind to allow yourself to understand the concepts I will teach you. I am going to share with you ideas that may seem very alien at this moment but somewhere within you, after you have had time to digest the information, it will begin to make perfect sense. At the very least the information will give you a different point of view from the norm and may make more sense than the traditional explanations that you are used to.

Here is a very bold statement that I am going to make to you. ***Whatever you pay attention to - your energy will flow to.*** What does this means? It simply means that whatever you are thinking about, or paying attention to, you are giving your energy to that person, object, or thought. Energy will leak from within you and go to that which you are paying attention to. Let me put this into perspective for you, just hang in there for a while before you start to question what I have said.

The Human Body is an "Energy Bank" The way you understand normal banking is that in order to be able to sign cheques and spend your money you need to have money in your account first. (Let's forget about overdrafts and loans, etc. for the moment). The same applies to the energy bank, your body. The currency is energy units and you must have credit of this currency within your body (the bank) before you can spend them. Relate it to any banking structure in which you need to put money into an account before you can spend it, either now or later. So how do we get credits into our Energy Bank?

The first way I am going to explain is when we are asleep at night. Through breathing, our body, our Energy Bank account, gets re-charged with energy. This energy also enters us through the membrane of the skin, as we breathe through our skin as well. This Energy comes from the Universe. It is our birthright and everything and everyone in the world has access to it. Don't ask me why or how? ***It just is***. I can't explain this, and remember this is not a scientific book to explain how things work. The Ancients in India knew it as "***Prana***", and in China it was known as ***"Chi"***. In the West it is known as ***"life-force"***. Please do not confuse this Energy currency with oxygen. It exists within the properties of oxygen. From what I have read, scientists have not been able to make sense of it.

When we are asleep at night our body gets charged up with this Energy so that in the morning we are all charged up and our bank balance is in credit. This may explain to you why someone of reasonably good health always feels their best in the morning. Ever heard the saying "I feel completely recharged after that sleep"?

During the day, because we have been programme to use our minds constantly through thinking, we spend our energy credits. Image that for every thought we have in a day we use one unit of energy. How long do you think it would take us to be in deficit of energy, assuming we do not recharge ourselves? If you went out shopping spending non-stop all the time and didn't put any money into your bank account, what would happen in the end? You would run out of money and would be in the RED, in overdraft. Effectively we would be bankrupt and the bank manager would start chasing us.

Now, what would happen if you NEVER stopped using your mind all day long? If your mind is in constant chatter, over thinking and worrying about absolutely everything from what to wear, what to eat, what did she/he say about me? Unsurprisingly, the energy units in your account would be depleting very quickly. Are you getting the picture? The more you think the more you use up your units. ***ENERGY WILL JUST LEAK*** and deplete from your Energy Bank. Those of us who are great worriers use our units up very quickly, maybe as early as mid-morning. Have you ever noticed that you get tired at certain times of the day? For those of you who are tried first thing in the morning you begin your day energy bankrupted! Tiredness indicates that you are running on a low Life Force and your Energetic Bank has low funds of energy/life-force. Let me give you an example of how a typical day might go. This is only an example as your own day may be different but is likely to have similarities in that you will be tired at some point. You are no different from anyone else; you have been conditioned and you will use up your energy.

Typical Day

"Life is about change, but growth is optional." Bruce Lee

When we wake up in the morning our Energy Bank balance is high with the energy credits deposited within us by the Universe the night before. We are energy rich. We may then get up; pull our curtains back and notice it is raining and perhaps make some comment about the weather. Here is where we start to deplete our bank as energy follows thought. We lose our energy to the things we give our attention to and so you can see, if we are not careful, we leak energy the second we wake up.

Next, we may decide to turn on the radio or TV as we go about preparing for work and as we hear bad news, and start to pay attention to it, we burn more units. We then receive our post and there is more bad news, we have overspent on our credit cards, more worry and so more energy being used up.

As we travel to work whilst reading the paper, or if we happen to travel by car, listening to the radio, ...guess what? More bad news is being delivered to us. Alternatively, we may spend our entire journey worrying or berating ourselves about our overspending, or wondering if the rain will stop by the time we arrive at work, or worrying about some other personal matter. This ***incessant chatting*** in our head never stops and drains our energy constantly! By the time we reach our workplace we begin to feel stressed out and are probably a little irritable. Imagine, we have not even started working yet!

My research has shown that ***STRESS is an indication that the body is running low on energy***.

When we are low on energy, our body begins to tense up; we get irritable, our patience is virtually non-existent, we find fault with most things, we become intolerant, things begin to get too much and the muscles in our body become tighter without us realising it until we experience pain. Think about your posture as you work at the computer all day. Have you noticed that your shoulders rise as you get more engrossed and worried about completing your work in time? After a while you may feel pain or stiffness and this prompts you to relax your shoulders down.

Everything in our day becomes a big deal; even the smallest of incidents often become over exaggerated and things may get out of hand. The tenser you are, the greater the body pain. These pains will materialise anywhere in your body, but the most common areas are initially the head, then in the stomach region, chest and back area. In some cases the pain will manifest itself in the knees and/or joints.

All this indicates that we are running on low energy and there is also an energy blockage within the body. When you become tensed, energy cannot flow easily and so a "blockage" results. Just like if a drainpipe is clogged up with garbage no more can pass through. It is important that energy is able to "flow" around the body, charging up all our organs.

The above describes how we continually lose energy all day and how "energy-expensive" our chatterbox brain is! We feel exhausted! Unfortunately, most of us do not take notice of our feelings or have never been trained to "read" our body, carrying on regardless of what is happening within us. We assume that this is how life is - painful! Nobody told us any different.

The sad part is that through our ignorance we have depleted our energy system and caused ourselves to be ill. The good news is that it takes many years before a disease will set in. Now that you have this material you can do something about restoring your energy balance before an illness becomes degenerative.

WHERE DOES YOUR ENERGY GO?

When you deplete your energy, you eventually become rundown and then "ill". ***The first sign of this is tiredness and then as things become worse you suffer from chronic fatigue, depression and finally a dis-ease.*** Here is another eye-opener for you. Every experience that you have had in your life is recorded within the cells of your body. Yes, there is a memory of every experience since childhood. Now, depending on the type of emotions that were created by your experiences, these will be recorded in different organs, including your bones.

The Ancients believed that all the different emotions were linked to certain organs. For example,

- ***Anger*** was associated with the ***Liver***,
- ***Sadness*** and ***depression*** with the ***lungs***,
- ***Worry*** manifests itself in the ***stomach,***
- ***Hastiness***, ***the lack of joy***, and ***cruelty*** are linked with the ***heart.***
- ***Criticisms*** and ***fear*** with the ***kidney.***

These are but a few examples but it is important to understand that every part of the body is associated with some sort of emotion. I can sense that some of you may be questioning this, but again I am asking you to hang in with me until you have finished the book. Don't make any judgements quite yet. So I will repeat again…***All Emotions are recorded within the body.***

Let's return to the typical day we may experience. We progress through the day losing our energy to the things that hold our attention most. Since we spend much of our time working, we lose energy to this, but also we lose energy when our mind over-thinks. Believe it or not, we spend the majority of the time thinking about the past or the future and we are never really in the present moment. Working with my clients has shown me that most individuals will spend their time in the past. We may think about what people thought of us; how badly we were treated; how we were betrayed; how angry we are with those who have let us down; how we are misunderstood; how unhappy we are with our situations; our jobs; our children; our partners; parents; how life is unfair; why me….., the list is endless.

Then, not being happy with our present situation, we begin to wish and reflect on how our lives could be ***IF ONLY…IF ONLY…***becoming jealous of other people's lives. Now, we have shifted our attention from the past to the future, and STILL NOT THINKING IN THE PRESENT! This constant chattering means we are leaking our precious energy units (energy follows thought) and so we feel tired. Furthermore, the above thoughts are what we call big expenses. Giving our attention to them causes us to lose high value units of energy and hence leaves us tired very quickly.

Do you know what your biggest energy expenses are?

Worry and Fear!

But this statement is vague as it covers many incidents and we need to be more specific about emotional categories. It is important that you are aware of the thoughts that you create in your mind, which cause a loss of energy. It is only by understanding thoughts that you will learn to conserve your energy, spend less and so begin to heal.

Research has shown that **Criticism, Revenge, Guilt, Resentment, and Anger are the most expensive energy burning emotions**. Under each heading there are a variety of causes, for example under "Anger" you could list not being understood, being abused, being betrayed, being abandon, and so the list becomes very long. ***As***

another exercise for your own reference in your journal, draw five columns and title them Criticism, Revenge, Guilt, Resentment and Anger. Under each heading write down the physical and emotional past events that were most hurtful to you and which generated these feelings. Some things you list may be duplicated in columns, try to identify the core. For example, under Criticism you might record events related to judging others, fear of being judged, not being good enough, or comments which criticise you for not meeting the expectations of others. Society expects us to have families by the age of 35, not be divorced, parents want us to be professional people like doctors, accountants or lawyers. Get the idea? Go on, do it now, make a start on it and during the next 21 days keep adding to the list and I will advise you what to do with it as we go along. By the way, the list that you generate will only contain a few events that you remember at a conscious level. There are many other events and behavioural patterns that you are not aware of; but even a little awareness is a good beginning.

Now that you have your list, study it. Can you see a pattern? Have you noticed that they relate to either ***Wealth*** or ***Health*** or ***Relationships***? In fact, all our problems can be broken down to these three elements. Try it, keep questioning yourself and the emotion and the cause of it. I am confident you will identify the primal cause to be one or a combination of Wealth, or Health or Relationships. Of course relationships are the "biggie". We have relationships with everyone that we come into contact with: our parents, teachers, siblings, bosses, lovers, etc. etc., in fact everyone and everything. So you should now begin to understand the big energy expenses in your life so let us move onto another topic.

WHAT HAPPENS WHEN YOUR ENERGY RUNS OUT?

Try and grasp this statement. When we are in credit of life-force/energy, no harm can be done to us. But incessant chattering in our mind, which is mainly past related or fear about our future, can drastically drain our source of energy. Depletion of energy can cause harm. ***Now, what will happen when the energetic body has used up all its quota of energy?*** It has to get energy from somewhere and where do you think it gets it from? The quickest way for our body to access energy is to borrow it from our organs, but there is a price to pay for going down this route. Your body parts will be weakened by this action and you start to feel "pain".

Other sources of energy are to be in silent meditation, rest, take a short break, have a nap, relax, do yoga, t'ai chi or chi gong, or just stopping what we are doing. ***These activities stop the chatting in our mind, cause us to breath slower and begin to relax.*** However, because we have busy lives and perceived responsibilities, we fail to do any of these and, in effect, we do not value ourselves enough to do them. ***This is what I wish to change in you. YOU ARE IMPORTANT. The most effective way to conserve your energy is to be in the here and now.*** Stop thinking of the past and the future, otherwise, unknowing to you, your energetic body will take over and borrow from the organs. Let me make it easy for you to understand by giving you an example:

AN ANGRY PERSON'S EXPERIENCE

Let's assume that there is somebody that you know who is an angry person by nature, who throughout the day has angry thoughts about their job or about what has happened to them in the past. They may have someone in their lives that has always let them down, abused them, or never respected them. As a result they constantly judge others, are upset by others behaviour and always expect to be let down. In short they are just a very angry person who has never been understood. Such a person will spend their day just burning their energy with angry thoughts.

What happens as they eventually run out of energy? Well, the chatterbox continues to work even when their energy is depleted! Now, understand how. Their physical body organs will supply this need for energy and in doing so they become weak. Just imagine for the time being that these thought forms of anger are being recorded in the liver. As a result the liver lends its energy to maintain the "energetic body" during the day in the hope that come evening it will be repaid through the Energy Bank when they go to sleep. ***The energetic body comes first and then the weakness starts in the physical body, bringing disease and illness.***

However, the energetic body is only capable of taking a certain quota of lifeforce at any one time. Also, since the person is a big thinker and worrier other emotions, apart from anger, trouble them during the day. This leads to other organs loaning their energy to support the emotions recorded within them. All this results in the life force gained at night needing to be shared amongst all the depleted organs and none being "fully recharged". This means that most of the organs, including the liver, are weaker compared to yesterday and since angry thoughts were most prevalent the liver will be the most damaged. Remember what I said earlier? ***"All emotions are stored in our body."***

Over a period of time this undetected activity breaks down the organs bit-by-bit, although this may take many years. Finally, in the case of the liver, a physical disease manifests within it as it is so weak from angry thoughts. If this "breakdown" is not attended to nor corrected, then over time the liver is likely to end up in a degenerative state.

Of course there are other factors that contribute to damaging the Liver. I consider these to be secondary, as I believe it is the loss of energy that is the primary cause. My conclusions come from my assessments of the hundreds of cases that I have worked with. In all cases where I have made my clients aware of their past emotional issues and where anger has been present they have all seen improvements in their liver function.

On a physical level we link alcohol and drug abuse with damaged livers. In fact, there are many things on the physical level that we consider to be the cause of our illness, including our environment. Again, I am not going to explain this as the medical profession and scientists have done a good job on this matter from their point of view, however, my purpose is to highlight to you an alternative perspective of how illness originates. ***My beliefs are that the seen manifests from the unseen, therefore, physical diseases manifests from the loss of energy.***

As a point of interest, just think of the people that you know who suffer from liver problems and that are drinkers and/or drug users. Can you now recognise that a majority of them are also angry at life? The above is only a small example giving you an idea of how the liver can be affected by the emotion anger. Now extrapolate this understanding to a larger scale and try to comprehend how other parts of the body become diseased through different emotional thoughts. ***Every part of the body that becomes diseased has an emotional story to tell from the past***. Again, this book reflects the majority of cases and not those that cannot be explained, for even the medical profession cannot explain everything. I am sure you will agree with me that my findings are making some sense to you even though they may seem "far out". Finally just to recap: All body parts and organs are subject to the ***"Energy Follows Thoughts process" and are connected to our emotional thoughts and feelings.***

PAIN IS OUR FRIEND

Now you are saying I have gone mad, ***pain is our friend…*** "How can you say that?" Everybody hates pain!! I know, just hold on a minute and carry on reading instead of jumping to a conclusion. Notice how we prejudge things without listening to the whole matter. This is our behaviour most of the time, making rash judgments, and so losing energy even in just reading a sentence in the book.

I say pain is our friend because ***Pain informs us that there is a problem and that we are running out of energy***. Now, if someone tells you that you have a problem, wouldn't you consider them a friend? Pain is a sign that there is a problem in your body's system and that there is an energy blockage. But how many of us really take notice of this message? Most of us take pain for granted; assuming it will go away if ignored or this is how life is to be, painful. Some of us are conditioned to take a painkiller either immediately or when the pain is unbearable, while other amongst us just carrying on regardless of the pain, suffering in silence.

Painkillers may give relief, but for how long? Though it may "kill" the pain for now, in most cases it will come back again, either in hours, days or weeks. This is because the ***pill has only addressed the symptoms and not the cause.*** So guess what…we end up taking pills again and again and again. I will be so bold to say that this is how modern day medicine works most of the time. Again, please do not make judgement if you do not agree with me…just carry on reading; after all, this entire book is about an alternative route to understanding yourself and I will, in the end, prove my point.

The sad fact is we probably give more attention to our cars than we do to our bodies. If there was a red light blinking on the dashboard in your car or you heard something rattling in your engine, you would take time out to have it looked into. This is because you know from experience that if you ignored the "symptoms" the car is likely to eventually break down and not work. ***I wonder why the majority of us will not take time out for our bodies?*** Quite simply it is because we do not value our bodies and do not consider them important enough. We fail to love our body and so ourselves. We are not appreciative of what the body does for us on a daily basis. We are not aware of the body's workings and assume that it works without needing any proper maintenance. Again, this is just ignorance as we weren't programmed to look after our body.

In conclusion of this chapter, again I will remind you that all body parts are subject to the "energy-follows-thoughts" process and are closely connected to our emotional thoughts and feelings. Through constant abuse of the system, disease will eventually reside in our body's organs. ***The good news is we do not get ill over night. It takes many years for the system to break down. The very good news is you can begin now to reverse the process.*** You are on a healing journey already by just reading this book. So STOP WORRYING about the past and what you have done to your body so far.

We Are All Addicts

"When you become immobilized by what anybody else thinks of you, what you are saying is that someone else's opinion is more important than your own opinion." Dr Wayne Dyer

The human being has the capability of becoming addicted to anything that it comes into contact with, both in the seen and unseen worlds. What do I mean by this? Remember the physical, material world refers to the "seen" and the "unseen" implies the emotional and energetic worlds. ***My definition of addiction is an uncontrollable behaviour for doing something either externally or internally to make us feel BETTER.***

An addiction is when something has power over our whole being and takes complete control over us. In fact, both worlds, seen and unseen are connected to cause and effect of this addiction. The feelings that we initially have are unseen and are so strong that they cause us to crave an external physical experience to satisfy our internal needs. Hence, it is our feelings and emotions (our cravings) that control us. So understand that everything begins firstly from within YOU, the unseen world.

When we know ourselves intimately, we begin to notice that our behaviour and emotions are linked and a series of patterns can be identified. Through our early conditioning we have repeated these patterns and through trial and error have learnt this behaviour from past experiences and from those who brought us up. The people we cared for, admired or even feared also influenced our patterns. These could be our parents, guardians, carers, friends, peers, siblings, or teachers. (I am sure you could think of a list of people who have influenced you. Please note these in your journal now).

We initially become addicted to these "patterns" because they generate feel-good feelings. We experience an internal feeling of pleasure from an external stimulus. Since we like this feeling, we repeat the pattern in order to generate more "good feelings". However, the more we do so, the more we enjoy the pleasure brought by the feelings experienced and so we repeat the pattern. The "pattern" takes control over us. The feelings control us. In some circumstances some of us have become addicts through FEAR. By this I mean we carry out activities because we want to please others, valuing others' needs and opinions more than our own. Completing such activities is likely to lead to people noticing us and the sense of importance this generates. For some, not doing what others expected meant being abused either physically or emotionally. Hence, sometimes when others' opinions are given so much importance, we end up doing things that we do not even like. We become addicted to the behaviour in the hope of gaining their approval and, at the same time, angry with ourselves for doing something that we do not like. We start to hate ourselves because we do not honour ourselves. In this case it becomes a vicious loop, a downward spiral. ***The pattern controls us.***

We also have the ones who didn't know any better and accepted pain as the only way they understood their worlds, and with these people pain became pleasure. If there was no pleasure and someone told you and changed the label pain to pleasure this would be your reality, wouldn't it? So here we have people who accepted pain as pleasure. These people unknowingly enjoyed being punished. Their pain was pleasure, as they didn't know any better. They are the ones that remain in abusive relationships until they learn differently and begin to have some self-respect, and when they do, they will move away from that relationship. When I talk about pain I mean ***physical and emotional pain.*** With emotional pain it is people that are tied to others by emotional blackmail.

The most common addictions in our civilised society are ***over indulgence in eating, shopping, drinking alcohol, smoking, over working, recreational legal and illegal drugs, gambling, sex, relationships, watching TV and leisure activities.*** Of course, there are many more that can be listed, (List yours and think what you are addicted to) but I would like to draw your attention to the following few to share my findings. Now, you are probably saying that this is a way of life for civilised society and from your point of view I can only agree with you. Nevertheless, from my point of view we are addicted to most of what is being offered and ***addiction is also a very costly expenditure of life force.*** The fact that the majority of us are really ignorant of what the loss of energy/life force could result in we unknowingly overspend our life force. Managing our energy has not been in our reality. Remember again I am giving you an alternative perspective of how to view life and the workings of your body associated with energy/life force.

In the previous chapters, I mentioned that we are bombarded with advertisements from the media making us feel inferior and that there is something wrong with our current situations. This coupled with our teachers of life has made us dependable on external influences. So, ***the message that is conveyed to us that we are not worthy and there is something lacking in our lives*** becomes loud and clear daily. It is as if what is advertised will make our lives more complete if we buy their stories and we will feel better afterwards if we bought their products. As a matter of fact this is true, it will make us feel better but for how long? Because of our addiction to feel good again soon, how long do you think it is before we repeat the pattern again? Again each individual is different and the time varies between each of us. We will definitely repeat these patterns in order to feel good. It is only a matter of time before it is repeated.

THE ESCAPIST

Through our early encounters in life, our initial experiences of pain and pleasure were clearly defined in our cell's memory. Memories of pleasure are always welcomed back, so we seek to have more of such experiences, repeating what gives us pleasure, whilst our memory of pain means we run away from it, avoiding it if possible and doing less of it. However, there are instances where there are no alternatives, no way out and we have to make a stand. We will counter attack.

With memory of pain in our pain zone, our cells will remember unpleasant situations we encountered in the past. These feelings will be remembered as "unpleasant feelings." (Feelings could be fear, sadness, anger, feeling unloved, unworthiness, restlessness, guilt, resentment, and boredom. ...Again the list is endless, you may fill in your list). From our first unpleasant experience we would register this as not pleasant. As we grow older and experienced more of this unpleasant experience and if we didn't like it, we may have wanted to run away from it or wished something else could make it right. This is where we began to consume foods or adapt some other behaviour patterns in order to feel good to hide the pains. Eating became one of the earliest addictions that we started with, and then shopping. As we experienced more of life, we found that we could avoid these painful situations, and in doing so we were able to create alternative behaviour patterns. We also found comfort in someone's company or engaged in some other activity to find comfort. Some of us did all of them to try to find comfort.

Some of us have learnt that it is possible to make a stand if we do not like a situation and may be aggressive to whoever inflicted the pain (either physical or emotional) on to us. We would argue, be violent, and shout back and this would for some of us give us a feel-good factor instead of running away from the situation. However, some people are the opposite and are quiet and passive. The person who is quiet finds feel-good feelings within the quietness. Most quiet people are quiet because they have been criticised so much. Every person is different; we could also do all the things that I have mentioned to feel good. And if we did nothing we would burn up inside with this feeling making us feel even worse and consequently we have to take something for it like pills or something stronger like alcohol. Guess what, this is part and parcel of your journey and when it takes control of you it becomes an addiction. Does it mean that there is no hope for us? Of course there is a solution. Just hang in there, we will get to it soon.

How does this addiction manifest? When there seems to be no possible solution to our internal situation at that time, we seek to escape and bring some comfort from being uncomfortable. Hence, the need to do something to make us feel better, like shopping, eating, drinking, smoking, gambling, or taking drugs; these are just to give you some of the hundreds of examples. I call these addictions/habits "treats". Unfortunately, these treats are not permanent fixes and as the pain comes back again, as it usually does, then we do more of our "addiction". (Most pain is two-dimensional, we experience pain physically and emotionally)

What do you think we are escaping from? I have mentioned this earlier; we are escaping from situations that are connected either with our ***wealth, health, and relationship with others and self***. ***We are not at peace within ourselves.*** The fact of the matter is, we are not happy first with our inner self. Remember what I said earlier regarding the unseen? It will always come first, but we are not aware of this because we have not been taught to look within ourselves. Everything is targeted to the seen, the physical reality. Being an addict, there is something within us that takes control of us to do these things over and over again, and we are not conscious of it, how can we be? It is internal and in the unseen, we have not been trained to be aware of what is happening within, we have not been educated that such worlds exist with us. All we are aware of are some feelings within us and it feels good or not good. Again, we think that everybody else is the same and that is how life is. ***What are you escaping from? What***

is it in your situation that is so terrible that you can't escape from? Go on, again write down your fears.

So let's recap, I said that we are all escaping from some internal pain (uncomfortable feelings) created by the external situation, and because we do not know any better we have found comfort in some form of addiction in order to cope. These addictions give us a feel good factor, and I also added that we become escapist because we are not at peace internally.

I sense that some of you are not in agreement with me. What do I mean by inner peace? Let me ask you first, what is your definition? Please take a moment and think about it and then write it in your journal before you read any further.

For me, inner peace means that whatever the situation that I encounter in any current moment, I am accepting of it. Acceptance of "WHAT IS" gives me inner peace. Think now what gives YOU peace? Do you know when you are at peace? Let me explain this further by taking some worst scenarios as examples. We can go back to the London bombing on 7th July 2005, this incident was really tragic, or even the attack in New York on September 11th 2001 where thousands were killed and injured, so many people were killed, how can I accept it? Shouldn't I be angry with the terrorists? Be sad for the families that have lost loved ones? Or what if I had personally lost a loved one or a friend in that situation? Wouldn't I have an emotional charge within me, like anger, rage, hatred, sadness, or fear? Of course, I will experience these emotions in me, but firstly, what can I do about the situation that has happened? If I lost a loved one who was killed in the tragedy, I cannot change anything. I cannot bring that person back. Nothing will bring them back, yes, the anger, emotions; etc. will be with me but the fact is I cannot change the situation of what has happened. The person is killed, gone, the incident has happened. Nothing can change it......So all I can do is accept what has happened first. So acceptance of ***"WHAT IS"*** is step number one. If I do not accept what has happened, I will lose more energy than if I accept. If I do not accept, I will go through the "what ifs" and "whys", etc. I will be living in the past. Being in the past will cause me to lose energy.

Talking about it, or thinking about, the whys and ifs, will not change anything. It has happened. The sooner I come to this realisation and accept what has happened, the better. I only have to deal with one less thing with the emotions. Even having to think of one less thing will save me some energy that I otherwise would have lost. This is only one of the many incidents and in this case a major trauma. But during the day we go through many other minor incidents and if we do not accept what happens can you imagine how much more energy we will spend?

Yes, I will have the emotional attachment that goes with the situations, and I have to deal with that, and you are saying there is sadness within me, or anger or any of the emotions that were mentioned, ***how can I have inner peace?*** You are perfectly right in what you are stating as you are reflecting your past experiences and conditionings that when something like this happens, we should be in a terrible space/situation. Something tragic has happened. We demand justice, explanations, and the whys of it. And more questions being asked. Somebody has to pay for the tragedy because we are hurt. We become the victims. We seek revenge. You are so right from your point of view as that is how you have been conditioned to think and I respect your opinions. Now can you see how by viewing the situation from your eyes you are using large amounts of energy? Please let me explain further.

Being in present time, in the NOW ***causes one to lose the least amount of energy, in fact, the very minimum*** Having accepted "what is", in this case the "tragedy", all I have left in the now are my raw, painful emotions. I have only limited choices with what I can do with them. Accept my painful experiences, not deal with them, or totally deny that they exist.

For some people not dealing with the pain is the easiest option because facing the pain seems too painful. Not dealing with it means you run away from the pain. And so we look to find comfort in something else to block out the pain or at least ease it. In the above example we may take to eating to comfort ourselves, or not eating at all, or hiding in a room, (reflect on your behaviour and see if you can see a pattern). This behaviour does not fix the problem; it only eases the discomfort for a while. Eventually, someone or something reminds us of our pain. Or we start to think of the situation again the past and we will re-enact the pains again.

When this happens we seek comfort again to escape and block the pain. In this instance we have used eating as the alternative. Supposing this does not sedate the pain, we may try something else, like drinking alcohol or shopping. We could then end up being addicted to several things over a period of time just over one incident. ***Eating is associated with comforting our uncomfortable feelings/pains and this is how our internal feelings begin to take control.*** The feeling comes first and if we are not capable of dealing with it, we then turn to comfort the feeling.

In the above example, in which I chose to give you the worst of scenarios, I hope that I have managed to make you understand how we can become addicts, creating our addictions through our non-acceptance of pain. So now you understand how an addiction is created, go back to your childhood and try and recollect the uncountable pains that you had and also list your compulsive and obsessive behaviour so that you may understand yourself better. ***When I say that we are not at peace inside, what I am saying is that we are not in acceptance of our feelings.*** The good news is if we pay all our attention to our feelings and accept this unacceptable pain and be in the NOW totally, coupled with deep breathing, the feeling will actually lessen. When you really pay all your attention to that feeling that is in your body and think of nothing else, the pain will subside. You will then begin to understand that pain will come and go.

When you are at ease with your pain/emotions, you will experience what inner peace means.

SOME OF MY EARLIER ADDICTIONS

I would like to share with you some of my earlier addictions. The earliest one, with exceptions of sweets, chocolates, fizzy drinks and ice cream, I would say was cigarettes. I must have been at the age of 12 when I first tried them and at a time I wasn't at peace with myself. My parents were fighting a lot and this must have scared me. As far as I can remember my home life wasn't a happy one. I also got bored easily and the combination of being scared and bored became my "uncomfortable feelings". Looking back I can say I must have turned to smoking to hide my feelings. Being also curious and noticing that adults do it, and with peer pressure, I tried smoking. I hated it. I didn't like the taste of smoke. How many of you really liked it the first time you tried smoking?

My "uncomfortable feelings" coupled with needing to be accepted by my peer group made me retry smoking and, over a period of time, I suppose I learnt to like smoking. This became a very bad habit. Of course, the nicotine also made my physical body a slave to it and I would smoke to feed the physical craving for nicotine. Not only did the nicotine have a control over my body; the feeling of acceptance that gave me a feel-good factor was associated with cigarettes. I gave up smoking when I was 50 years.

Boredom played a very big part in my early life. It was a trigger that got me addicted to so many things. As I got older, I also didn't like being alone either, this also gave me an uncomfortable feeling. So I then tried drugs, booze and eventually gambling to comfort me. All these habits gave me a feel-good feeling and helped me escape my inner turmoil. Of these, gambling was my biggest problem. Gambling gave me a buzz, a thrill, the excitement and the buzz was greatest when I won. This good feeling was so powerful that in order to maintain the high I would gamble more to repeat the euphoria. I had to keep winning. But of course, this wasn't possible because you will have winning streaks and of course you will have loosing streaks. The feelings controlled me all the time so that when I was on a losing streak, I would carry on in the hope that I would next hit a winning streak. Of course this always ended up in disaster, as I would run out of money and finally get into debt. And to make matters worse, when I ran out of money, to hide the pain and guilt I would drink or take drugs and this was a vicious circle. So for a short time in my early lifetime I was just working to feed all my habits. Isn't it sad? I was at such a low point of my life and I had no money and plenty of debt. There was only one way out and that was to stop. I had to stop because I didn't have any access to cash and, to cut a long story short, I was dragged kicking and yelling by my loved one at the time to Gambler's Anonymous (GA). I had no choice; she was going to leave me and refuse to support me in any way if I didn't give up. GA stopped the gambling for a while with its buddy support system but it didn't deal with the feelings of unrest in the inner self. Of course, not knowingly other addictions were created to replace the feelings and gambling.

So every time I needed comfort, I would turn to one of my many habits to seek the comfortable feeling. Shopping and working long hours replaced the gambling. The need to shop helped to relieve the uncomfortable feeling but I needed money to shop to feed my habit, so I ended up working long hours in order that I could shop, plus all the other habits that are not mentioned. At least this time, whilst I had a new habit, I had something to show for it. The fact of the matter was ***I wasn't at peace with myself I was looking for external things to make me feel good inside.***

Having developed the habit to win through gambling, I became very good at my work because I had to win at whatever I was doing. And as I progressed in my earlier careers in life, I was successful at whatever I put my attention to. Although I wasn't gambling at the tables or the bookies, I was gambling with life. I had to win in life. This was fortunate for me because the more I worked at my businesses, the more successful I became at the time, but I was still fuelling my habits. The more life disagreed with me and gave me uncomfortable feelings, the more I would shop and work harder. This was my escape. Outsiders thought that I was a hard worker and responsible and that I was happy in what I was doing. In a way I was happy getting comfort from my external world, but my internal world wasn't happy, I had unresolved issues, which gave me uncomfortable feelings, and I would use the external world to escape the feelings. ***You can see how easily we can get deceived.***

I got pleasure from winning at business, at sports, winning the approval of my father, family, friends and loved ones. I found out that money and power went together and I liked this new feeling. I found a new pleasure giver and a big new addiction. I was addicted to power and money and it hid my real feelings. Makes you think of the many powerful people we look up to out there, eh? Are they really at peace inside?

In my circle of friends I had to be number one or try to be. I had the latest gadgets, cars and furniture, most expensive holidays and weekends. My children went to the best local private schools. People admired me. I had won respect. As I became more affluent, my habits got more expensive. My wardrobes were full with the latest designer outfits. I was the envy of most people. To them, I had it made. I seemed happy externally. I was fortunate to retire at 45, but was I happy inside? You know the answer to that. As you can gather I was consumed by habits to hide my pain and it was a vicious circle. You can now have an understanding of the people who have everything and are habitual shoppers. Do you think they are really happy inside?

Please write your habits down. It will allow you to understand yourself better. Be honest with yourself and try to spot the less obvious ones, not just eating and shopping. Try and find the more subtle ones. I have tried to share with you how some of my addictions started, but many have not been listed. What I have tried to do is to show you that because we are not at peace in life we escape our emotional pain by creating our habits/patterns. I would like you to take a moment to reflect back on your own list and try and understand how you created your habits. Habits linked to memories you may not want to recall. Your conclusions will be the same as mine that you are not at peace inside.

HOW DO WE FIND THIS INNER PEACE?

I have learnt from experience that by total acceptance of "what is" and being honest with my feelings, I could initially find some peace. By staying in the NOW, the present moment helped me further to be in touch with my uncomfortable feelings. Being mindful and just breathing into my uncomfortable feelings subsided the intensity of the discomfort and finally put me at ease. This allowed me to be calmer and more peaceful inside. With continued practice I learnt that I could eventually be peaceful even when I started off being uncomfortable. I could, through acceptance, change the situation. I was in control of my uncomfortable feelings and when I realised this, I also realised that I wasn't losing energy big time. ***I became a good manager of my energy bank.***

Of course, there have been many instances in my life where the situations weren't to my expectations and I wasn't in agreement with what happened. There have been situations where I may have judged something as being incorrect, unethical or immoral. But what I have learnt through my past experiences is ***whatever happened I could not change anything, but I could change my feelings about it.*** I could turn uncomfortable feelings to ease. I had the tool. Through this understanding I have come to give this book the title "***It's OK NOT to be OK.***"

HOW DO WE CURE OURSELVES OF OUR ADDICTIONS?

First recognise that you have one, but we have so many, some physical, some mental and some emotional. Most people think that their behaviour is acceptable and normal. And that is normal, but what is normal? I have spent hundreds of hours with clients suffering from some form of addictions or other and we have gone through hours of pain and counselling dealing with the victim, the attacker, the abused, the dissatisfied, the betrayed, the abandoned (these are only a few of them) that lives within them. We are addicted to a substance, a drug, a person, and a habit because we are running away from something, and we find solace in whatever it is that gives us some degree of comfort at the time. So what happens next is that we like the feeling from the habit so much that we repeat it in hope of re-enacting those same comfort feelings again.

When we are uncomfortable with the pain, either mental, emotional, or physical that we are experiencing in our life situation, we will move away from pain and find solace in a habit that will free us from the pain and allow us some comfort. With repeated occurrences of the habit we soon become addicted without realizing it. In short, all addictions are a substitute for being loved. i.e. LOVE. Everything we do in excess is a substitute for love. Even in the beginning when we experiment with whatever it is, it is because we are separated from love. For example, in being bored we do not know what it is that makes us bored, but actually we are looking to be loved. If we felt love we would be complete. We would feel good and we would not lack anything. Remember I said in the beginning that love would heal everything. We would be running on a very special energy, you might call it high-octane life force. It is so powerful that it will refill our bank with new life force. Our inside will be at peace. Oh no…what am I doing to you now? You challenge this now! Well, sit back, close your eyes, relax and say to yourself 30 times over and over "I am love"…what do you feel? You will definitely feel different. I know you cannot say that you felt nothing for I know that when you mention the word 'love', there is power to it. I don't know how or why, but it just does. So just bear with me for a while and be open to new information.

All forms of addictions take us out of present time. It drains us of our lifeforce. Whatever you pay attention to, your energy will follow.

Energy follows thought. Very seldom are we in the present moment, and it is in the present moment that we can cure ourselves of any addiction or illness. Strange isn't it. As I said earlier on, you have to know that you are addicted before you can change a habit. The only reason you will not change is because you are fearful or ignorant of change. Admitting to ourselves that we are in need of help is the first step towards a cure. Now you want to know how to do it. Very simply, release yourselves from the past. How? I will explain that later. I suggest that you do not try to go to the chapter on healing your habits yet as you will miss lots of valuable information. For now, just be aware of the habits that you have listed.

You Become What You Think

"The key is to have a dream that inspires us to go beyond our limits." Robert Kriegel

"You become what you think", another very bold statement I am making. Just keep an open mind. You will soon learn to reason differently. It is just another way for you to look at things. Remember, I said earlier that the unseen (energy, thoughts, emotions) comes first before the seen (physical). And if you follow the process, you will accept that we are the creators of our reality through our thinking process.

Take a moment out and recapture your thoughts over the past few hours. And these are only your thoughts in those few hours and there are thousands……… Can you imagine if I asked you to think back over the last few days, weeks and years? What thoughts did you have then? Millions. I am also sure that you were either in the past, or in the future, making comparisons, or in most instances making judgements of others and self, or worrying about what people thought of you. You were either having a conversation with yourself or with others or justifying your situations. Worrying about your life, your duties, what to do next, planning your next move. (These are such high-energy expenses). ***You were never in the present. Are you ever???***

And yes, you have to plan for the future, but don't dwell on it all the time. Think about it, make your plans and then forget it and review it as and when necessary to check whether you are on course. Set your goals for the future and work on a daily basis correcting your course towards your goal, but be in the present whilst doing it.

We like being in the past, because it is comfortable, it is safe, and we know it. If we had unpleasant experiences in the past, we will try to avoid these in the future if we can. If we had pleasant situations, we will keep repeating them because they are safe. So, ***we tend to repeat the past most of the time in the present.*** Through our thinking of our past we create our present. We become what we have thought.

I usually illustrate this with my clients with a carpet in the middle of the room that we are working in. The carpet is about 2 meters long by 1 metre wide and I say to my clients "Imagine that this is all of you. If you never change, this is the size of the carpet. All your thinking patterns and behaviour patterns are within the carpet. That is all you are; ***you are your past****"* Within the "carpet" (life) we would repeat what was comfortable, and what wasn't comfortable, we avoided some things, as we liked to be in control of our situations. We like to be in control, don't we? Let me tell you that being in control means that you are stuck; not venturing out of your carpet, only repeating what is within it. Your carpet will never grow. ***So your past is always your future in the present***. Nothing changes, because you are not prepared to step out of the carpet. Stepping out of the carpet means taking chances, allowing yourself to move out of your comfort zone, and making your carpet larger. The more chances that you allow yourself to take, the more new experiences you will have and this allows you to grow. Being in control to me means that you are afraid of changes and your future will be your past in the present.

What usually happens when we think about the future? We are either escaping into the future through daydreaming and creating lovely situations about the future if our present situation is uncomfortable, or giving ourselves a hard time thinking how unsafe the future is, creating fear in our minds. If we go into the ***what ifs***.........or ***if only***...we will only stay stuck as we will only choose situations that are safe to us, and we will only repeat the past in the present through thinking about the future.

So our past becomes our future because when we play it safe, repeating what we know, seldom will we venture out because we have learnt through conditioning that change is scary. So we are not prepared to take chances. We create illusions about our future that are so fearful that we will not go forward and will revert back to the past where situations were safe, hence we go through the loop again. Most future thinking is fear based as the unknown keeps us prisoners of our thoughts. We imagine things that make us uncomfortable and therefore we stay within. This "F E A R" I would describe as ***False Evidence Appearing Real.*** It is in your mind and is not real and is only an illusion. The only thing that is really real is the present moment where you are, anything other than that is an illusion. Allow yourself to step out of the carpet and grow in your experiences of life. Again we have become what we have thought. If you are one that is a goal setter and takes chances and loves changes, you know what the rest of us are going through. (You would have stepped out of your carpet many times over and your carpet will be growing all the time).

Most of us do not take chances because we are afraid of failure. Failure is frowned upon by our society. Somehow we have been conditioned to feel ashamed or unworthy if we do not succeed (Not succeeding means failure in our society). So the easy option for us is not to do anything but stay stuck on our carpet, it is safer. It is better than failure because we have learnt from our past that failure gives us uncomfortable feelings and sometimes we are made fun off, scolded or humiliated. Success means being praised and rewarded. Success does not happen the first time we attempt something. So when we do not succeed the first time, does it mean we have failed? No, We just didn't get the desired outcome. However, if we keep practising we will get the desired outcome in the end. Remember the first time you rode a bicycle? Were you able to ride it without falling off?

So our programming is, ***success equals good feelings*** and not succeeding means feeling bad. Did you notice that I used the words not succeeding and not failure. Not succeeding is that you did something a few times and it didn't produce the desired result you wanted. That is all it means. And if you are prepared to try and try again, you will get the desired result in the end. We have been programmed that not succeeding equals failure. If you think that failure is bad, then you will always be afraid of the future and trying anything new. If you change your thinking that not succeeding is only not getting the desired result, and with adjustments to your plans and by trying again, you will get another result. It does not mean failure. Another result would be success or not succeeding. And if you do not get the desired result again, you try again. This way you will not stay stuck.

Every invention that was ever invented began from a thought. And through the thinking process the idea was manifested into the physical world. Let's take a stool for example. Somebody had to think of a stool first. So the stool came from a thought (unseen). Then we make it through trail and error and finally succeed by making the stool (seen). It does not matter how long it took to make it. If we decided to make more stools, the 2nd and 3rd stools will be made in less time. As we start to make more stools the making time further reduces as practice makes perfect. Such is the refined machinery that we are as humans. So if from our thought forms we create things, then it will be logical to assume that our thinking process can also cause us to become "dis-eased".

In the earlier chapter I explained how, through ignorance, we deplete our life-force/energy and eventually become bankrupt and have to borrow from our organs. Through constant abuse of the system we cause our organs to break down and eventually become diseased. Our chatterbox never stops talking and in the process drains our energy and causing us to become ill at some later point in our lives. So would you not agree that by following the logic I have presented to you, it makes sense to conclude that we ***create our illness?*** Now some of you are really annoyed with what I have just said. How dare

I suggest that you are responsible for your illness? You being ill is the luck of the draw in life. We are victims of our circumstances. Again, if that is your point of view I have to respect it. Let me explain further and perhaps you may have a change of heart about what you have just thought.

The information given to you about Energy medicine is way out of your understanding of the norm. So again I ask that you be open-minded and allow the thought that we create our illness to stand for the time being. If we create our illness we can also create our reality. The good news is, if we create our illness, can we not also un-create it? Hmmmmm, that has made you stop to think. Yes, I am saying that if we created it and made ourselves ill, we can also make ourselves heal by reversing all that we have done in the past. We just have to do everything the opposite of how we used to do things. That is to CHANGE. Those words again ....***CHANGE,*** (step out of the carpet)

If our dysfunctional behaviour and thinking patterns have bankrupted us, do you think that you could be solvent again if you changed your patterns? Of course, the answer is yes. It is like any business. If the business is spending too much, you cut down your expenses. In this case your excessive thinking and behaviour. Let's put it to the test. Again, what I am going to share with you is based on actual results that have been shared with hundreds of my clients. The majority of them have had success, had more energy and their ailments have healed, but there are a very small percentage that didn't heal and sadly, some even passed away.

There is no guarantee and there are lots of things that can't be explained as to why some people heal and others don't. Even the medical profession hasn't one for this and they have a licence to kill their patients. If they treat somebody and that person doesn't respond to their treatment and dies, it is perfectly acceptable. These people end up being some statistic. It is totally acceptable to the public. But if an alternative practitioner happens to try to heal someone who is ill and the person doesn't pull through, there is inevitably an enquiry. Their head is demanded on a plate. Does this seem fair? It is a fact that more and more people are turning to the alternatives around the world to be healed. Have you wondered why? The fact is, people are waking up to the issue that drugs have side effects in the long term and are prepared to try other alternative means. More people are prepared to take responsibly for their healing instead of leaving it to doctors and drugs. Also it is a known fact that more and more people are having successes through the alternative route.

My whole point in writing this book is to teach you to heal yourself without drugs. It is about practising preventative medicine. ***This is a "how not to get dis-eased" programme***. You now have to put me to the test and see how differently you will be in the end when you have tried my teachings. But before we do that, let's learn more about energy management, without you learning to run your energy correctly, it will be difficult to heal.

Energy Management

"There is no security on this earth. There is only opportunity."
General Douglas Macarthur

In any business for it to be successful it depends on good management. I am going to teach you to how to manage your energy efficiently and stay healthy. First of all we have to learn ***how to lose the least of energy***. Remember that energy follows thought.

So the first thing you have to learn is to be ***in the present.*** By being present I mean just that. All your focus is in the NOW. The mind is mindful of being in the now, in whatever you are doing. It is not thinking of something else. If you are preparing your meal, your mind is totally with the preparation of the meal, if you are eating your meal, your mind is with you eating your food and savouring every mouthful. In fact, the mind is not thinking; it is just still. This is why meditation is so good for you; it stops your monkey brain. I suggest you learn some form of mediation to still the mind. Remember, "How do you eat an elephant?" Start off with a few minutes per day and build up. Let's start with one minute first and even then you will find it difficult to still your mind. When you get good at it you can learn to do the waking meditation, which is being totally with what you are doing most of the time in your awaken state, being totally mindful. When you are in the present and quiet you lose the least amount of life force. In fact, I believe that when you are still and in the present you are being charged up with life force. Research has shown that people who do yoga, chi gong, or any meditation practices feel much better after they have done it. Their bodies are relaxed, they feel no stress and their energy is flowing through their bodies.

Here are some simple rules that you can follow. They are both simple and difficult because of your current conditioning. You don't know life to be any other way.

Stop Judging: We spend lots of time making comparisons between things and situations; we are either judging others or ourselves. ***Learn to accept situations as they are and 'let it be'.*** These are high expenses. Judging others means that we are unworthy ourselves and see flaws in others that really we have within ourselves. Otherwise how would we recognise them? Another new concept to grasp. It took me many years to understand this one. ***"You see in others what is in yourself."***

When we finally find no faults within ourselves we will not be able to find faults in others, so the simple rule is to accept yourself more. In fact, don't just accept yourself, love yourself to bits. This is the difficult part. ***Loving YOU unconditionally***. Accept all of you. By accepting all of you I mean, ***accepting the good parts and also the parts that you think you don't like and would term them bad***, I would rather call them the good parts and the opposite parts of you; not bad. When you use the word ***bad*** it means something negative. Now you are learning to look at words and change the labels you previously had for them. There is no such thing as good or bad, there are only opposites. If all you knew was "white", you would have to experience what "black" was to appreciate white, but does that mean black is bad? No, it means that black is opposite to white. ***In all our experiences in life there are only opposites.***

You will also begin to understand the power of words. Soon you will learn to understand more and will appreciate that ***others are mirrors of yourself*** and that they are in fact your teachers. But I don't expect you to buy into this at the moment. As you begin to understand energy more, you will understand that everyone that you come across is a potential teacher. You will miss the point of the lessons, as usual, until you love yourself more and stop judging them. They will always reflect something back to you of yourself.

Stop needing to be right, the need to win, having to prove a point! We use up lots of energy winning arguments or wanting to win. Again, accept 'what is'. There is no need to win. Why? What is it that you need to prove? That you are better than the other person? If you need to win, then there is an issue you have to sort out internally with yourself. You have got a self-esteem problem with yourself. This is a good time to go inside you and find out why your self-esteem is low and then put it in your journal. Why is it that you need to win? Why do you have to be better than the other person? Would you rather win and have a degenerative disease or not win and stay healthy. In my earlier chapter I mentioned that through abusing our life-force we will eventually become ill, winning all the time consume lots of our energy and eventually one of your organs will become diseased. I know which option I would choose. ***By not winning it doesn't mean that you are wrong or a bad person.*** You are just open minded enough to accept what has been said without judgement of right or wrong. You have allowed somebody to express his or her opinions without judgements. You can then move on conserving your energy.

Accept another's opinion to be right but not the truth. Allow others to be right in what they are doing or saying. From their reality, whatever they are doing is the correct thing for them, although you may not agree, from their point they are right in choosing what they are saying or doing. Let me give you an example: If somebody said that you are " X " (stupid, fat, ugly, lazy, etc. fill in the gap) and you know that you are not, let them be right. Why give any of your precious energy to that statement? In defending or needing to be right you are wasting a whole load of energy, and what for? Just because someone, in his or her opinion, thinks that you are whatever he or she perceived you as. As long as you know that you are ***not*** e.g. stupid, don't buy their stories. When you really accept who you are and love yourself unconditionally, you will not take any notice of what anyone says. Even if it isn't true, you will agree and move on. ***Never let someone impose his or her beliefs on you. Don't buy their stories. Just listen and don't react as you know who you are.*** I know that this is difficult to master but if you want to stay healthy, then this is what you have to learn to practise.

How many times have you made judgements of others? And no matter what anyone said to you, you have stuck to your guns to maintain that whatever your beliefs are they are correct. Of course they are from your point of view. I have learnt to accept everybody's point of view and allow them to be right. That way I conserve my energy. I have learnt to let everyone be who he or she wants to be. What right have I to judge? It is about accepting "what is". It is about having loads of energy in your bank and staying healthy. It is not about wining or losing. Winning would cause me to use so much energy and I don't want to be winning and be ill in the future. ***People that need to win or make a point are very insecure inside and have a history of ill health.*** Make a list of your argumentative friends and also the control freaks. You will surprise yourself by finding out about their health; most of them are not healthy people. They have a health problem. Here we have another bold statement, and it is so true. And if they are not ill yet, watch this space.

These people need to be right; they need to show off to others by making others feel small. These people usually have very low self-esteem themselves and are bullies. By bullies I mean that these people force their will on others and want to control them. They need to put others down to make themselves feel good. They have no respect for others; but the real truth is that they have no respect for themselves. If I am pressing your buttons, then you better stay with your feelings and learn to be still instead of lashing out, as per usual. There are many unresolved issues within you. Again, you are not at peace and you are using an external influence to cover your inner pain.

Stop trying to change others. We spend so much time trying to change other people when it is we that need to change. ***It is our expectancy of how we perceive our life and how others should react to us***. Have you noticed how often you are disappointed? It never goes according to your plans. If it does, it is only for a short while. When it doesn't go according to plan, we get disappointed and go though the motions of getting disappointed. After this, resentment sets in and the monkey brain goes into overdrive doing its usual of judging etc, causing you to lose plenty of life force. It is much easier to change yourself than to change others as most of the time you don't really know how they think? You think you do, but you are not in their bodies. Again it comes down to accepting 'what is'. If you think that you know how they think then you have programmed them to think that way and you have conditioned them. You are a control freak and a bully and the other person is a pleaser. ***Accepting 'what is'*** will keep your energy level high and ***when your life force is working, your immune system will do its work.*** You will be dis-ease free.

Learn to mind your own business. Over the years I have learnt that it is no use trying to help others if they are not ready to face their challenges. Yes, I know that once you find that you have had success with this you will want to help your loved ones and friends. Beware, most of them will not be appreciative of it as they think that you are intruding into their personal lives. I know that your intentions are honourable just like mine were, but you will waste energy trying to justify your cause. Let them be, ***allow them their right of wanting to be ill***. I know that it is difficult to just take a backseat and watch them get worst, especially people who are close to you. Until they are ready, they will not change. So the best thing is to be there for them when they are ready. You just change yourself and by your example, they may notice some differences in you and may ask you for your help. Some people may not like changing and resent it. You need to be strong in allowing them to be who they are or you will be bullying them to be as you are. Help ***the ones that ask for help.***

The above are some tips on how to go about your business daily; the message that I am trying to get across is to accept 'what is'. Let go of your expectancy. ***Expect everything and nothing at the same time.*** So when you expect nothing and when something happens, you will be pleasantly surprised. My life is full of surprises and I have learnt about letting go of my expectations and accepting ' what is'. Try it. At the end of the day you will find that you will be less tired, you are less stressed and you are beginning to get to know your body better. You are now a manager of your Energy Bank and can look forward to a healthy life. Yes, this is the beginning. We are eating our elephant bit by bit.

Remember:

- ***STOP JUDGING***
- ***STOP NEEDING TO BE RIGHT***
- ***ACCEPT ANOTHER'S OPINION TO BE RIGHT***
- ***STOP TRYING TO CHANGE OTHERS***
- ***LEARN TO MIND YOUR OWN BUSINESS***
- ***ACCEPT YOURSELF UNCONDITIONALLY***

Understanding Our Spirit And Ego

"Suffering comes from needing things to be different. When you stop that, your suffering stops. You can want things but it is needing them that must go." Dr. Wayne Dyer

In the previous chapter I said that you become what you think, if that is the case, then we should be very careful with what we are thinking all the time. Don't you agree? If we could create our realties, our illusions, our fears, our illnesses, and again there is a whole host of things that we have managed to do to ourselves, the list is endless so it is only sensible that ***we should start to think differently*** and create a better reality for ourselves to live in. Try and catch yourself thinking negatively about yourself and ***change the thought***. You can always change your thoughts by saying "I choose to think differently this time."

I also mentioned that the unseen comes before the seen, energy comes before matter, therefore matter manifests from energy (Einstein's theory) and so the physical body manifests from the energy body. Earlier, I also mentioned that we are energy beings first and then human beings (In this instance I would like to change the word ***energy to spirit***). The ego, your physical being is the sum total of all your experiences up to date. You are your past. So, being unconscious and having been programmed that you cannot be anything else except being physical, you can only repeat your past because you don't know any better. ***Your EGO controls every bit of you.*** You are your EGO, and if you are your EGO then what is your SPIRIT?

Ok, tighten your seat belts now and I am going to give you information about your SPIRIT that will blow you away. But before we start, let me ask you one question first. ***What do you think is the purpose of your life?*** Go on write it down in your journal. Most people in the civilised world think that life is about having 2.4 children, getting married, going to work hoping to get a good career, earning lots of money, having a couple of holidays a year, having a nice home, good relationships with partners and people, giving love and being loved, and of course good health and a happy ending. That is the ideal life for most people, and if we happen to be poor, in dysfunctional relationships and our lives are in a real mess and not going according to our expectancy of life, we tend to bitch at how cruel life is all the time. Saying to ourselves" if only we………. (fill in the blank please), our life will not be so bad. What is it we have done to have all this bad luck" etc. etc……….know the story well? I bet you do.

Did you know that your SPIRIT is that part of you that is far superior to your physical being? Just to show you a comparison of how different your ego and spirit are try and imagine that the Stone Age Era is your physical being and the modern world today is your spiritual being. This will give you an understanding of how far apart they are. ***Spirit is total love and has no concept of fears or time*** and can only reside in your physical body when you are perfectly still or in the present (that is when your life force is the highest). When you start to think into the past or the future, that means the EGO has taken over and your Spirit moves out of the way and the EGO takes over. EGO and SPIRIT cannot occupy the same space (your body) ***yet.*** I use the word ***yet*** because when you are unconscious i.e. not aware of your Spirit, it is not possible to occupy the same space. When you are aware of who you are and what your purpose is, the Spirit and the Ego will eventually then be one. But for this to happen takes lots of practice of being conscious of your thoughts and being able to heal your past and letting go of fears from the past and those of the future. In short you have to put your EGO to death. By death I mean loving it to death and changing most of your lifestyle and thinking. When you learn to let go of your expectations in life, and learn to let go of fears, your Ego will die slowly and you will begin to grow more and love yourself more. The more you are in present time, the more you will understand what the marriage of Spirit and Ego is about. At this moment your Spirit is seldom within you as your Ego is in control most of the time. Remember what I said about being in control? That is why you are depleted of energy and Spirit is not within you.

The Spirit has no sense of right or wrong on its journey, whereas the Ego has a whole set of boundaries that belong to correct or incorrect procedures. The Spirit is limitless and has no boundaries. It is infinite. The journey of the Spirit is forever, there is no end, and whereas the journey of the physical has limitation, about an average of 70 years on this physical plane, Spirit is energy and cannot be depleted. It cannot be destroyed. ***This is a scientific fact. You cannot destroy energy***. Therefore the journey of the Spirit goes on forever, it goes from one journey to the next, from one body to the next. When the physical body dies, the Spirit just moves on to the next body. The Ancients knew of this and to them this was known as reincarnation. Again I am trying to make the explanations very simplistic, there are again hundreds of books written on reincarnation.

It is fact that the physical body dies but the Spirit doesn't. You have a choice here and if you think that you are your physical body, then at the end of your physical time there is only death and no more. If you believe this, like millions of others, then you will want to squeeze every ounce out of this lifetime. You will want to try to be in control of your life and you will want to get the most out of this lifetime. Or if your life is so terrible, you may be bitching all the time and may want to end it by committing suicide many times. We all would like to create our life "to be perfect" the way we would like it, like a fairy tale story. So we end up rushing around to do as much as possible, punishing our physical body unknowingly. But the sad fact is, how many of us have achieved this life known as the perfect life? Do you want to know the truth? Very few have achieved this state.

Without knowing you personally but because you are reading my book, I know that most of your life has been a constant battle of disappointments and fears. You have reached a point by asking yourself certain questions like, what is this life really all about? It is not going according to your plans….. Remember that I told you earlier you that you have been sold a story that you are never good enough and in order to be acceptable you have to be what your group, the public or the media, recommends. You have no faith in yourself and have given your power to external influences. WHY? Because you do not love yourself, yes, I am stating that and it is true no matter how you are trying to justify your situation. ***YOU DO NOT LOVE YOURSELF UNCONDITIONALLY.*** Sure you may say you love yourself but there is a string of conditions attached to your love, and what do you actually mean when you say to someone ***"I LOVE YOU"?*** Go on write this down in your journal.

When I say, "I love you" to someone I mean that I love them for who they are and accept all of them totally. I accept their good and also their opposite parts. I have no judgement of them whatsoever. I accept them unconditionally. To get to this stage one has to accept oneself totally first with no conditions and this will take time and ***constant practice of identifying your patterns and healing your pains***. I know that it has taken me many years to come to this understanding through my own searching journey. In the past my love was full of conditions, and if you didn't conform to one of the conditions, I would have taken it as I wasn't being loved. Of course, I was constantly being disappointed because of my expectations and conditions. When I learnt ***to let go of my expectations and accept 'what is'*** I began to understand what unconditional love meant. To be unconditional with others you have first to accept every aspect of yourself and this is difficult to grasp and understand. As you read on it will become clearer to you.

THE JOURNEY OF OUR SPIRIT

If this were the only life, then we would wish to have the ideal life that I mentioned earlier. Good health, ample wealth, loving relationships and everything being just perfect according to your expectancy. How come we don't have it? Isn't life cruel, if this is the only life that we have, then we should have the best! Why does it not happen to all of us? Why are most of us so miserable? Why is there so much misery in this world? If there is a God up there, it is an unfair God, why are we victims? Why can't we have a good lifetime? I used to ask these questions when I was a little boy. Why were my parents always fighting and why couldn't we be a loving family? As I grew up I had more questions, and the more I asked, the bigger the victim I was. Life was just unfair. Most of the time I was always disappointed because life didn't turn out the way I wanted it to. Can you resonate to that? Yes, although I was very successful at business and I had ample amount of money, there was still something missing. That something was inner peace. I was looking outside all the time to find it and of course it wasn't there. I was looking in the wrong direction like most of us, until I woken up by my misfortunes, but it wasn't a misfortune, it was a blessing in hindsight. At the time, when things didn't go my way I thought I was a victim.

There is a reason for the way things are. There is an order that orchestrates our worlds but our human minds cannot comprehend the workings of this great Universe. Remember I gave you a comparison of the human and the spirit. From the human aspect we can't accept that there is some orderly fashion out there that controls everything. It is because we don't believe that everything is in perfect order that we need to be in control. We think that this is the only life there is, so we have to do as much as possible as time is running out on our physical life. There is a limitation to it.

Life Is Not What You Think It Is

"Smart people learn from experience. Super smart people learn from other people's experience." John Bytheway

Let me blow your minds more with what I am going to share with you. ***Life isn't the way you think it is supposed to be.*** There is much more to it than seen by our physical eyes. If there is no more to life and it is just some hit and miss chance that we were born to be who we are today, then most of us are victims, and there is no justification for us being here. Why should we be born to all this misery and pain? Why couldn't we be born into a better existence?

There is a divine and greater plan, and the reason you are here is because you chose to be here now. Your Spirit has decided that. Now I am beginning to annoy you because if we chose to be here, then why have we chosen such a bad existence? Again, you are perfectly right in what you are saying because the proof so far is that life is not good and you are a victim. How dare I suggest that you chose to have all this pain! Again, allow yourself to be open-minded and absorb this alien information and your life will begin to make more sense to you and the purpose of you being here will begin to have a meaning.

I used to ask myself, why did we come into this physical plane to suffer most of the time? Why was there so much pain and suffering? Why didn't life turn out the way I wanted it to be? The more 'whys' I asked, the more 'becauses' I had, and I had hundreds of 'becauses'; more reasons but none gave me a good answer. I finally realised that I was also asking the wrong questions. The question that I should have asked was, ***"What am I doing that I am attracting this situation into my life now?"*** By asking this question I really had good answers and they began to make sense.

I also found that the more I tried to control my situation, to have it my way, the more matters would go against me. Yes, sometimes it would go in my favour for a while and I would be happy for a short time, but in the main I was always disappointed because it never turned out the way I planned. My inability to accept ***'what is'*** caused me most of my disappointments. Through years of bitter experiences and pain I learnt that until I was ready and able to accept 'what is' and was prepared to let go of my expectations, stop resisting 'change', trying to fix my life and other peoples' lives, that I finally did learn that there was some order to my chaotic world. Amidst the madness of my world it was really already perfect and that there was a real purpose in one's life.

THE PERFECT TIMELESS BEING

I want you to imagine for a moment that you are this invincible being that lives forever. You are this super being (like superman in the comic strips) that cannot be destroyed and your life is just one great adventure. You have no concept of pain or pleasure. All you know is love and nothing else. You know you are already perfect the way you are. You love yourself unconditionally and you know nothing else but love. You can do anything and as you are already perfect, you have no understanding of right or wrong, and your beliefs are whatever you did was perfectly acceptable. You live in this timeless world, never ending and your whole existence is one never-ending journey, travelling from one body to another, one planet to another, from one galaxy to another from one sun to another. You can become anything you want and can experience everything that is available for you to experience. In short, your world is your oyster. You have access to every part of the universe and can be anything. Now imagine that you are this being. What will you do? I know what I would do. I would try everything. I would experience all that was available to me.

In order to have these experiences, imagine that there is this great library (The Hall of Experiences); it is huge, bigger than anything that you could imagine. This great big library has every book on every experience that one could encounter, there are trillions (if there is a word bigger than this then it would be that word) of books all containing different lives and experiences that you could lead and experiences you could have. Experience different emotions, different sexes, being in different times and this goes on forever. Right now, your human mind cannot comprehend what is available. To bring it to your level of understanding let's say you could be a male, female, son, daughter, husband, or wife. You could be a king, a pauper, a strong person, weak person, sickly person, or healthy person. You could choose to die at any age and of any disease in the physical world knowing that you would only come back again in another time and another body to again experience whatever you wanted to try out next. You could be a killer, the victim, the rapist, the thief, the whore, everything that represents 'badness' in your physical world, or you could be everything that represents the opposite, the 'goodness'. But really there is no such thing as good or bad as they are just opposites. You are this being that wants to experience whatever that is on offer as you know that there is no good or bad, they are just experiences. ***You really have nothing else to do***. You are this timeless being, not able to be destroyed and you have all this timelessness on your hands. All you can do, and only do, is to entertain yourself through this timeless, never-ending journey.

This 'Hall of Experiences' is also accessible to the trillions of other beings that are around. Each and everyone knowing that they are also perfect and have nothing else better to do than to try out what is available in this library. The aim of course is to try out all that is available as there is no time limit. Let's imagine that you have got one of the books out and around you are also many other people all reading about different experiences. You may happen to be intrigued by the experiences of being abandoned and betrayed and wondered what it would be like to be a victim. So you ask one of your mates (fellow timeless travellers) around you to inflict these experiences onto you so that you can experience these feelings. Some of your mates agree and decide to be the ones that inflict these experiences on to you in a particular lifetime. You also agree that in another chosen lifetime you will reciprocate those experiences that were imposed on you. A contract is then agreed upon by all of you spiritual beings.

For example, one "mate" would say that they would be the father and would abandon you at a certain age, and another would say that they would be your lover and would abandon you when you are married. Or another would say that they would be your child and would abandon you when you are old. This is only a few of the thousands of experiences that one has in a lifetime. There are so many thousands of scenarios being agreed upon and contracts signed by so many timeless travellers during one lifetime. All this has been agreed in the unseen worlds. It is like a sophisticated 'flow chart', there were endless possible scenarios that you could have thought of and every action that you took led to somewhere. It was either full of possibilities or none. All this really depended on what you decided at the time of your journey in the physical plane.

This physical world that you look forward to coming to and have human experiences in is an exciting place for you. It is where you can experience 'the human emotions', and you cannot wait to arrive to fulfil your contracts. Now imagine that in any one physical lifetime there are many stories and many travellers involved. Again, I am trying to make it simple for you to understand, but rest assured that this plan that I am trying to put across to you is only a crude version of the real thing. Remember the comparison of the human and the Spirit?

So, in the unseen a very complex plan has been designed for a lifetime of experiences in this physical world. You have chosen your parents, your partners, your jobs, your co-workers, your clan, your children, in fact everything that you will experience in your physical life now has all been planned. Yes, you have planned your life so well. Also in your plans you have many combinations and computations for you to experience, it has many alternative plans in it as well. Nothing is left to chance, everything is already arranged and contracts with every other timeless traveller has been agreed upon, the roles each and everyone plays, the experiences that are going to be shared by all of you and an agreed length of time in a particular lifetime. This is also then connected to other lifetimes that you all agreed to play out and your earthly journey has been arranged for a certain amount of time. When all contracts have been finished you start the process again from the 'Hall of Experiences' plotting the next adventure with other timeless travellers. And this goes on forever, never ending..........You go from one lifetime to another, one experience to another, and one body to another body in the physical world. Your journey on earth is just one long journey. When you have had all your fun (yes, the journey is fun when you have nothing else to do) here you then move on to another world, another galaxy, and another system.

Once all contracts have been agreed in the unseen worlds, you forget what the contracts were when you arrive in this physical world to start your journey to have your experiences. You do not remember anything that has been so carefully planned when you arrive as a human being in the physically world. Upon your arrival you even forget that you are a spiritual being. You only know yourself as human and nothing else and experience the experiences of what you have set out in the unseen. So we come down to the physical plane having chosen our parents, partners, and our life situations.

If you look into your own experiences of your life, now you can have a sense of what I have been talking about. Your life up to date has been a myriad of experiences and is that of a roller coaster, full of highs and lows, and most of what you have experienced you do not like. Some of the experiences you have classified as really nasty, and ask yourself how on earth could anyone have asked for such terrible experiences; and some of the experiences you have had are nice ones, you try to repeat them. Being human you forget who you are and try to have only the nice experiences and avoid the nasty ones (but they are not really nasty, just opposite of nice), and guess what? ***The ones that you are fearful of and try to avoid keep returning back to you.*** Do you know why you keep attracting these situations? It is because of your fear of change. Being a human we have been conditioned to fear change and we stay stuck and dissatisfied with our situation and asking why…why are we in this hopeless situation? We think that if we change, we may hurt so many people around, or we may be afraid of the unknown and therefore we do nothing and stay stuck and complaining, all the time being in our comfort zone and becoming ill, thinking this is how life is. Life is not going to be like this all the time. I have some good news for you.

WAKE UP CALLS

The good news is, all of us have set up times in our lives on the physical plane to get wake up calls. These wake up calls are for us to remember, at certain times, that we are spiritual beings on a journey. I personally must have had several wake up calls during my lifetime and I wasn't aware at the time that they were wake up calls. I also didn't like changing much and I was attracting the same situations back to me, and I was always looking outside of me to make me happy.

I suppose it wasn't until I was fifty years old that I must have written into my plans to really shake me up because I ignored the previous warnings and I was given a very harsh lesson. Remember I told you earlier that these harsh lessons would come either through loss of someone very special, having a terrible disease, or loss of wealth? I was stripped of my wealth and that was when I was forced to change and look inside me. I then looked at my life seriously and asked myself what my life was really about. It was at this point that I started to let go, accept 'what is' and changed. When I didn't resist changing and let go of control and my expectations, I began to learn the valuable lessons that I am sharing with you now.

One point I would like to stress is that if I had still ignored that wake up call at 50 years old, it would also be OK as I would have probably carried on being very unhappy, broke, blaming life and definitely died of some terrible disease as I would have depleted my life force. Perhaps I would have also written into my contract that if I didn't chose to wake up then, I could also experience extreme pain, disease and discomfort and lived in that hell of unhappiness being human and forgetting that I was a Spirit in the physical plane. I would have died in my physical body thinking that this is the only life, not being able to let go or change. It would seem to be a terrible existence from the physical point of view, but ***my Spirit would have had such a wonderful experience and would have carried on with the next adventure in another physical body, enjoying the experiences of being human again.***

This is why I said to you earlier that you should mind your business, because ***you do not know the journey of that person, and whatever happens to that person is actually all right***. It is difficult when these people are so close to us like our parents, siblings, lovers, children or close friends. Actually, their spirit is having a great time, but the physical human is having some terrible experience according to our perception because we don't understand, and again don't forget that the Spirit does not actual feel anything, it just experiences 'what is'.

I would like to end this chapter with this thought for you. ***You are already perfect and have come down to this physical plane to experience human experiences. Do not forget that you are spiritual beings having human experiences***. I am sure that this makes more sense than the story that you initially believed about how life is. The mere fact that you are reading this book tells me that you are ready to accept change and new ideas. The fact that you are still reading and got this far tells me that you are seeking answers for your situations.

Finally in closing this chapter, always only give advice and assistance to the ones that seek help and ***PLEASE, mind your own business if they do not seek your help***. Just watch them suffer and know that they are brave souls that have come down here to have these experiences. Just love them for who they are and respect their journey. I know this is going to be difficult, as we all want to help those that we love but unfortunately we don't know their plans. I have been disappointed so many times with my own family, now I just stop trying to change them and let them be and carry on with their own journey, even if it seems that they are suffering. If you see them as humans, then yes they are suffering. You have to learn to look at them as spiritual beings having human experiences, and of course not forget that you too are a spirit first and that your life is also a journey. ***We are all kindred spirits on this wonderful timeless journey enjoying everything in our path.***

What Does The Awakening Mean?

"Our Misfortunes or Bad luck are an indication for our wake up calls" Arram Kong

I have now been in an awakened state for nearly 13 years. By awakened state I would say that I have been on a conscious path, more aware, alert, alive, active and definitely having more action. I am very conscious of my every action. You could say that this is the spiritual path. Looking back I have seen the vast changes that I have gone through and this didn't happen overnight. I am even today still learning as I find out more about myself each day and I don't think that one will ever stop learning. When I first encountered my worst nightmares 13 years ago, when everything that could have gone wrong with my life did go wrong, I was very angry at life, the world and God, and I hated everything. I hated myself most of all and my life. "Why me, why is my situation so dreadful, what have I done to deserve this? This can't be what life is about, why is life so cruel?"...etc. etc...I wished that I could have the good old days back. Even if the good old days weren't good, then they were certainly better than the ones now. You may very well be familiar with this record.

The reason I am sharing this with you now is to 'forewarn' you that when you next find yourself in a no-hope situation and are very fearful and angry with your life's situation and feel that all is lost, then that will be the time when you have set yourself a wake up call. When you are in a space that you consider a living 'HELL', that is the time when great changes will be possible for you, but you will be fighting change all the way. Eventually, when you learn to let go and face your fears and are willing to change, you may then find your purpose and your spirit. Mind you, it won't be that easy, as you will be fighting all the way with your old patterns and beliefs. This is only natural for you and all of us who begin to be awakened. At least now you will be aware of what to expect and how you could react when it happens to you. I didn't get that help or information when it happened. I didn't know that I was being awakened until many years later.

The good news is somewhere in the most dreadful times of your journey, you will definitely receive a message through mysterious ways to help you awaken. This message could be delivered to you through a friend or stranger or via the oddest of circumstances. The message that you will receive will not make any sense to you at the time, and because you will be so low at the time, you will not take on board anything. Perhaps you reading this material is the message! You will be sent to see someone, visit some place, read a book or to do something that is not in your normal behaviour and you will do whatever you have been advised to do. This is one of your opportunities to change. On the other hand some of us may do nothing and stay stuck, which is also OK, as I have explained in the previous chapter.

My message came to me when I was at my lowest. I happened to call round at my ex-wife's house to visit the children when a mutual lady-friend was there visiting my ex. We had not seen her for about 8 years but had kept in contact by phone and the reason that she called round that particular November evening was that the weather had turned foggy. She had driven her friend from Glastonbury to Heathrow airport and was on the way back but the weather was so bad that she had to stop over in London for a while to wait for the fog to lift. So she decided to visit my ex. During her visit we had the opportunity of exchanging pleasantries and exchanged news of what had been happening in our past. I told her about my "misfortunes and bad luck" and how I felt very bitter towards life. She suggested that maybe a break in the country for a few days would do me good. She was very insistent that I go down to Glastonbury for a few days and stay at this guesthouse where she was working.

Being financially embarrassed, the last thing I wanted to do was to spend money I didn't have and drive some 110 miles to a place I didn't know called Glastonbury. To cut a long story short I went to Glastonbury against my better judgement. Something inside me insisted that I go. I don't know what it was; it was illogical at the time.

When I arrived from London after a three-hour drive, I was tired; disappointed with the place I had come to and wondering what on earth I was doing here in this part of the country in winter. The house was cold and looked very uninviting on this dark evening. I had supper, had a hot bath and went to sleep. In the morning I woke up and went down for breakfast. There was nobody around expect for the lady who owned the place. As she prepared breakfast we made polite conversation. She asked me what I was doing down in Glastonbury and I told her that my friend, who worked for her recommended that I come down for a few days rest. She told me what was on offer in the guesthouse. This was a holiday place that offered massage, healings and meditation. She recommended that I have a meditation session as it would help me with my problems and make me more relaxed.

MY FIRST ENCOUNTER WITH 'UNCONDITIONAL' LOVE

I agreed to have the meditation and, to my surprise, she was the one leading the meditation. It was an 'open heart meditation', by that I mean she talked to that part of my body and opened my heart. All I remember was that she was talking and I was listening and I was asked to close my eyes and imagine I was good friends with my heart. We sat very still for what seemed like a long time but it was just minutes. In those few minutes I seemed to be in a different dimension or world. I felt so much at peace when I was sitting within my heart. I felt energy that I wasn't aware existed, and she told me that this energy that I was feeling was 'unconditional love' coming from the universe. Of course, being a very sceptical person I took all this with a pinch of salt, but I could not deny how I felt. I really felt so relaxed and at peace with myself. She then told me that I would be a healer and teacher in the years to come and that all my upsets to date were a sign for me to give up my old ways and start on a new path.

Can you imagine what I was thinking when all this was said to me? I really thought that this woman was completely mad. Anyway, as I was in a very good relaxed state, I thought I would just enjoy the atmosphere that I was in and ignored the ramblings of an old fool. When the meditation was over she also told me that I would be attending a healing course that she was holding in two weeks time as that would be the start of my introduction to healing. I asked how much it would cost for this Reiki class that she was holding and she told me that it would cost £380 and it would take three days. Furthermore, I would have to come back to Glastonbury and stay to do the course. All in all, this would cost me some £500 including my lodgings. You can imagine what I thought of all this. Me, spending money I didn't have, becoming a healer, and having to travel some 110 miles again in a couple of weeks time. I told the lady that I would definitely not be able to come as I wasn't interested in healing, I was a businessman and at the moment I could not afford the time or the money. In fact, I cut short my stay and went back the next day to London. I was furious at my friend for recommending me to go and also having to listen to such nonsense from a complete stranger who I thought was barmy.

During the next few days after my experience I felt very calm, I don't know what this woman did to me, or what I experienced, I felt really good inside, I felt such peacefulness amidst my huge problems. I felt good about myself even though I was in a situation that seemed impossible to get out of. Somehow I felt safe and OK. It was such a strange experience. I was always thinking of what had been said to me regarding being a healer and how ridiculous this was. You may be surprised to know that I was back in Glastonbury doing the Reiki Healing course. I did a deal with the landlady, who I later found out was a Reiki Master (A Reiki Master is a person who initiates a novice student to become a practitioner and healer). I came to some arrangement for paying for the course by instalments and I was initiated to become a Reiki Practitioner.

That weekend was so special and I will never forget it. I felt so much unconditional love with the people that were doing the course and saw many things in the unseen worlds. I felt energy come through me and out of my hands and I felt very light, very peaceful and happy. The three days passed so quickly. During the three days we would listen to our Reiki Master and do healings on each other. We were all novices but we were able to heal. How this happened I don't know. As far as I was concerned all this was beyond my logical brain and I was happy to be witness to something so extraordinary. I felt very good about myself and even my situation didn't seem to bother me too much. My finances were poor, but I was happy. I couldn't understand what had happen. It was as if something had been lifted/shifted inside me. It was as if someone or something told me that I would be all right. All this was very reassuring, but in the reality of things, I wasn't all right. I was broke and I had my creditors chasing me for money and I had no business or job but I had a new profession; I was now a healer. You can see how the universe had guided me through my friend, whom I hadn't seen for years, to set me on my new path.

I was so taken in by all this healing and felt so good that in the following months I went down to Glastonbury almost every weekend to help with the guesthouse. I did some cleaning, gardening or tidying up or walking the dogs. I did all of this for no pay. I just wanted to be in the atmosphere that my Reiki Master created. I was beginning to like the country life. I loved the energy that was around my Reiki Master and I didn't mind doing the chores for her. I had no job, and I had "signed on" for income assistance. Being on the dole and housing benefits did give my huge ego a dent, but I was grateful at least for what little the government was giving out at the time.

Whilst I was playing 'the spiritual role' I still had all my baggage with me from my past life. I was just as judgemental, angry, resentful, and vengeful. I was even judging all the people who were "awoken" and were also healers. Being a healer, I wanted to be the best healer; I was again in competition, needing to be the best. I really hadn't changed that much, but I had changed a little. I was slightly better than before if I had "woken up". I felt much lighter inside than before. ***You may also begin to feel that you have all the answers after reading this book, but don't let your ego fool you. For this is only the beginning of your journey.***

In the years that followed I was motivated to study many other courses. I learnt reflexology; I trained to be Taoist teacher to learn about sexual energy, I did t'ai chi, chi gong, and yoga. I spent two years studying iridology and graduated at the London School of Iridology. I trained as a 'Heal your life Louis Hay coach' and also became a Reiki Master. I have visited the USA frequently in the past three years to master 'Emotional Freedom Technique' with Gary Craig and also spent time with Eric Pearl in Europe learning about 'Reconnective Healing'.

I welcomed the millennium 2000 by isolating myself from the outside world. I was on my own for three weeks in my room just being in meditation and having no food. The first week I didn't have any food and water, and the second and third week I only had water. The 21-day process wasn't about fasting; it was about allowing and total trusting. It was about learning to tune into higher vibration levels, which allowed me to be sustained by Cosmic Light (CHI OR PRANA). I was very moved by an Australian lady called Jasmuheen, who instigated me into the process. She had been living on 'cosmic light' for many years and still does. She has not eaten any physical food for many years.

Having gone through the 21-day process I intended not to eat for the rest of my life, however, this didn't happen. After living on nothing for about three months I decided to go back to eating as this lifestyle put a terrible strain on my social and private life. I could not go to dinner parties and when people found out that I didn't eat, I was a threat to their reality. They have never heard about this process, maybe you haven't either. There are currently some 10,000 plus in the western world today that do not eat and just live on 'cosmic light' and they are very healthy and happy people.

My life's situation wasn't good to begin with and I was learning about myself every day. As each day passed I became a better person, changing a little bit at a time each day. The process was a bit like a diamond being polished. It has taken 13 years to get this diamond shinning brighter. During the early stage you could say I was just a lump of coal.

I started my healing profession one year after having learnt it, and that was an interesting time in my life. In fact I was healing myself as well as others. All I did was put my hands on people and I got some positive results. People were recommending others and the ones who had good results, and wanted to help friends and family, requested that I initiated them into Reiki. Because my lifestyle had changed, my needs varied as well and I didn't need lots of money to live on. I lived in my sister's home and fortunately at the time my outgoing expenses were very little. I had come to an arrangement with all my creditors and they agreed to a settlement figure over my debts on what I had offered. It was either that or I would become bankrupt. They chose the route of having some money rather than no money.

HOW I RID MYSELF OF MY NEEDINESS

Through going to different courses and reading lots of books, I began to have a minuscule idea about what my journey was all about, but I still had all my huge old baggage with me. I have been through many relationships during the past 13 years, as I was still a needy person, although I wasn't aware of it consciously at the time. As each relationship ended I learnt more about myself. Yes, I was still needy, but I was more aware of this behaviour within me as I progressed through each relationship. As each relationship ended, I went through my patterns of being needy; I experienced betrayal, abandonment and rejection stages each time. I didn't learn my lessons fast as I was repeating them over and over again with different women.

The only way that I could get rid of my neediness was to love myself more and not depend on someone to love me, or I to love someone. It was during this time, after I had finished a serious two-year relationship that one of my ex-girlfriends told me that I should really be on my own for a while. I hadn't been on my own for any length of time since I was divorced. In fact throughout my whole life I was always in and out of relationships or marriages.

This was the very best advice that I had received, although our parting at that time was again very painful. She noticed my patterns and my neediness and that was one of the reasons she ended our relationship, as I was getting too needy for her. I wanted to be married to her; this is just a case of ownership as in my mind I thought that the piece of paper would make everything all right. How sad I was then and this was only some 6 years ago. She was more mature than me journey wise, and the last thing she wanted was some needy person in her life. As she could not fulfil my obligations by getting married to me she ended the relationship. I was really stopping her progressing on her own journey. In parting she advised me that ***I should learn to be alone, on my own by choice*** and not really looking to be in another relationship because I really didn't love myself or at peace within myself, and if I wanted to be a better person than previously, ***I should learn to love myself more.*** Of course, during that time I was again screaming and shouting as I again thought that I had been betrayed, abandoned and rejected.

She insisted that when I really learnt to like my own company by choice, I would learn more about my patterns and myself. Most importantly I would learn to accept my company more and would love myself more each day. She also added that when I was OK being alone, then the right person may come into my life, but before that happened it may take a few years of suffering being alone, and being OK with this. As it happened she did me a great favour and yes, I have learnt to love myself much more unconditionally. I really do thank her now, but at the time I was very angry with her. We are still very good friends as we do care about our journey and swap notes on how to get through this apparently difficult journey. It is not really difficult, as it is us that make it difficult by our refusal to accept 'what is'. She is also a healer and counsellor and has her own cross to bear from her past.

I was alone for a couple of years and in those two years I learnt to accept and love myself more and was aware of my many dysfunctional patterns. Yes, the old habits were there but at least I was aware of them. ***Not judging others and self and being in the present was one of the most difficult things that I had to overcome***. It took many years of practice through self-discipline and watchfulness of self. It is during these years where all my techniques were developed and I think I have the process perfected, as anyone who has problems will be able to self-help themselves through this work.

LEARNING TO BE IN TOUCH WITH MY FEELINGS

The most important thing that I learnt was that I had to ***acknowledge all my feelings and to be aware of them at all times***. During the past 13 years, I have been coached by many spiritual teachers, books and experienced many painful events to come to this vital understanding. I learnt how to spend more time with my feelings within me and through being with these feelings and accepting them, I found that I could access the stillness hidden behind those feelings. ***I began to understand that in the event of every chaotic state I encountered, I could access the calmness through accepting the situation and dealing with my feelings.*** This lifted all the heaviness that I had experienced in the past before being awoken.

When one accesses this stillness one is actually in one's heart centre and one feels and has a sense that everything is all right even though it may seem at the time not all right. Again, it is difficult for you to comprehend what I am trying to describe to you right now as this is all alien to you because I am describing a new skill. You will not be able to access this process until you learn to be in your heart centre and be totally with your feelings. Then you will know what I am talking about. When I mastered being with my feelings, and when I came across situations where I would normally react by judging and causing myself stress (my old behavioural patterns), I would now respond differently. I became more aware of what was happening inside me and when I remembered that I could be with my feelings and learn to accept them, it dissolved the pain that came with the feelings and circumstances. It made accepting 'what is' easier. In the years that passed I managed to develop many techniques, which I have used very successfully with my clients. Once they have learnt the techniques to deal with their feelings, they could help themselves and didn't have to come back to me for more treatments. Obviously, the ones that had major problems had to come back to see me more, but eventually they managed to learn to heal themselves. Using these techniques correctly, I promise you that you will rid yourself of all your aches and emotional pains and you will be a much happier person, and learn to live one day at a time to a very ripe old age.

The Process "Chi Integration"

"No one can make you feel bad about yourself without your consent" Howard Wight

You have been waiting patiently, going through the previous chapters wondering how you could heal yourself and I thank you for being patient. I would also add that patience is one of the great skills that you have to master in the future. You will be confronted and tested with learning patience time after time throughout your whole life.

What is Chi Integration? It is a simple breathing technique where we consciously breathe continuously, without pause, in a circular or conscious connection breath, transforming the body, mind and spirit. The in breath is intentional and the out breath is relaxed and this creates waves of energy in your body that you can readily feel. The waves of energy massage and caress you from the inside. Simultaneously, the waves carry valuable information to you from your subconscious.

Many Ancient spiritual mystery schools have used this simple breathing technique to access non-ordinary states of consciousness for healing, and to reach union and connection with creation. Today we know and understand how the breath can open the subconscious to allow entrance to levels of stress, memories, and emotions held in the central nervous system and organs, which have previously been beyond the reach of conventional talking therapies. The breath enables us to release negative thoughts, beliefs and feelings that do not support our way of being. It unblocks any energy blockages created by our negative thought patterns and behaviour and gives us the freedom to allow more love, peace and joy into our lives.

I want to remind you that this is a proven method from the Archives of Ancient Taoist Masters in China. I am so fortunate to have been a student of a modern Taoist Master who spent most of his early life translating the ancient scripts. The breathing method was an integral part of the movements and disciplines of martial arts and was a very important feature in healing and also strengthening the organs and mindsets. It was also a very useful tool for relaxation and meditation. I have simplified this technique to suit our modern style of living and have taught this technique to hundreds of people in the past. They have managed to rid themselves of negative emotions, physical pains and diseases, and are now living very balanced healthy lives. Hopefully when this book is available to the public there will be a greater awareness and it will help many more.

To be good at anything you have to be disciplined and take your progress one day at a time. You have to develop skills like having patience and endurance. To be good at anything, you have to spend time practising and practising. Remember, "how do you eat an elephant?" It has taken me many years of researching and practising on myself and clients and I believe this is one of the easiest, simplistic and most effective methods of healing yourself and dealing with unwanted emotions.

Here are a few rules you have to master before you start.

STEP 1: BASIC TRAINING

- You have to learn to ***be in touch with your feelings when you are upset***. By this I mean getting to know ***what is happening inside your body.*** Be aware of when your heart rate rises, when it is beating faster, stomach churning, stomach cramps, the lump in your throat, the hot flushes, hands sweating, breathing faster, or literally not breathing at all, holding on to your breath. You will be surprised how many times you hold onto your breath. When anxious, people do not breathe at all or they do not breathe uniformly, they make the out breath longer than the in breath. Your body starts to twitch, you get fidgety, or you start to tense up; and finally you notice physical pains in your joints or body. All these signs are informing you that you are beginning to become fearful, stressed or angry. The situation is not going according to your expectations and you have gone into judgement of 'what is' and not accepting of it. ***These signals from your body are informing you that you are not comfortable inside and that your energy field is disrupted and unbalanced. You are not at peace and losing your life force energy.***

- As soon as you are aware of your feelings and physical activities (twitching…etc.) place your full attention to that part of your body and be with it for a moment. Now take an intensity count immediately. This means that if you are very troubled, stressed, nervous, angry or fearful, whatever your emotional state is at the time and the number 10 being highest and zero being lowest, (very calmly try to gauge where you are). If you are not so tense 3-5, fairly tense it may be 5-8, and very tense 8-10. If you are not sure what your readings may be, just guess it. There is no right or wrong answer in what you are doing. It is about having the experience of knowing what is happening inside you. Once you have established your intensity reading, start to breathe in and out very quickly for around thirty counts; this should take about 20 seconds. Then, retake the intensity count. It should be lower.

- Next, take long breaths in and out. Being a newcomer, you will probably be able to breathe in and out for about 3-5 seconds per time, that is 3-5 seconds for the in breath and same for the out breath. You can breath in through your nose or your mouth. Do whatever is comfortable for you but try to take longer breaths (After years of practice I am able to breathe to the count of 15+ in and 15+ out, but it took me time to get to this stage). When you are doing your breathing, and you do this for 30 counts of long breaths in and out, you also say to yourself in your mind or aloud, ***"It is safe to breathe***" repeatedly whilst you are breathing in and out. When you have done your 30 counts notice how you feel and how differently you are now. Notice the subtle changes that are beginning to happen in your body. Notice what is different in your body, and also take another intensity count. By this time you should be more relaxed and the count will be lower. ***If you don't feel any different, go back to the beginning and repeat the basics again***. In most instances where people need to repeat the basics, I know from my research that they have managed to shut themselves off from their feelings and it will take a while of repeating the above steps to get them to be in touch with their feelings again. Don't give up, eventually something will happen, my research has proven that through persistence you get results.

That was the first part of your training. Now go and write down in your notes what you have discovered about yourself. What differences did you notice within your body? What new experiences did you have? And lastly how much did the intensity count come down by?

STEP 2: AWARENESS TRAINING

- Having noticed what your new intensity count is, this should be a lower figure than what you started with, start paying attention to that part of your body that has a sensation. Breathe quickly again for 10-15 counts in and out within 10 seconds, and then start the slow breath breathing at about 4 + counts in breath and then 4 + counts out. Keep this going for a few minutes and increase the counts to longer breaths, if you can, as you do the exercise. Whilst you are doing the breathing I want you to say to yourself,

- "Even though I have this feeling (e.g. of anger against X for having scolded me), **I am willing to accept myself unconditionally**," and if you are comfortable with that, you can change it to,
- "Even though I have this feeling of XXXX, **I accept and approve of myself unconditionally**." Finally if you are comfortable with this statement, you can change it to,
- "Even though I have this feeling of XXXX, **I love and approve of myself unconditionally**."

- You need to be breathing and saying this statement to yourself at the same time. When your breath gets longer, you will start to notice something different happening inside you. You will become calmer and the feelings may move to somewhere else in your body. Your muscles in your back and shoulders will begin to relax more. You may get tingling sensations and sometimes you may have pain. Don't worry about the pain as the more you breathe into it, it will subside and eventually disappear. Feelings can also be emotional or physical. Keep track of the feeling wherever it goes and when you feel that the feeling has subsided, you may stop the process. Next, think about the incident again, now you may retake an intensity count again of how you feel.

You repeat the above until the intensity count comes down to as near zero as possible. When you have accessed this space, you should really be getting very quiet inside and totally calm.

- ***RETESTING:*** Think again about the incident that you started this experiment with. How do you feel about it now? Is there a difference from how you felt the first time you thought about it? You should be feeling different now from the first time that you thought about it and the intensity count should be much lower compared to the first time. When you definitely feel better about the incident that happened to you, go on to the next process; if not, go back to the beginning and start all over again until the intensity is very low compared to the first time. That was quite easy, wasn't it? Also very painless. Again, go and write down what you noticed has changed inside you and your perception of the incident now that you have done the process.

STEP 3: THE FORGIVENESS & LETTING GO TECHNIQUE

- Now that you know how to come to achieve this calmness through breathing and affirmations, I want you to sit very quietly and place your attention to your Heart Centre. (This position is where your sternum is, between your breasts). Place your open palm (either hand) on the centre and say to yourself, ***"I forgive anyone that may have caused me to have these feelings and I also forgive myself if I have caused them"***, you should be breathing long breaths in and out now and saying the statement slowly to yourself or in your mind for about a minute. Then you add by saying, ***"I ask my cells in my body to let go of the memories of this experience." Repeat this, a minimum of three times.***
- Finally, just close your eyes and when you are in this stillness, just imagine that a bright light surrounds you and the light is coming from the Universe. You stay in this situation for as long as you want and try to be very quiet mentally, ***if you cannot still your mind completely, just let the thoughts come and go paying no attention to them, just watch the thoughts come and go and keep up the deep breathing.***
- When you are in the quietness, you will start to experience new things. This situation that you are in will be total stillness. You are aware of what is happening around you but you are not involved. You will understand what just being the feeler is, sensing what is around you and not giving any personal attention to it. There is no judgement within you in this

instance. 'What is' ....is, and that is totally OK, and what happened a few minutes ago happened. Your reaction to all that has happened is now historical. It has no hold on you right now. You are at peace with yourself and 'what is', and you don't react to it any more. You are not losing any energy and are totally calm and accepting of what happened.

STEP 4: BEING GRATEFUL TECHNIQUE

Finally, being very quiet and still and in your Heart Centre, you will say,

"I am grateful for the experience I have had and I am grateful for what I have in my life.
I am grateful for the food and shelter that I have and also for the petty cash on me in order that I am able to purchase things for my daily existence.
I am not aware that I am better off than 80% of the population in the world and that there are billions who are in a less fortunate situation than me.
I am grateful for what has happened to me, even though it didn't turn out as I expected and I found it difficult to accept 'what is', but when I compare myself to others in the world that have so very little, I realise that I am truly blessed in spite of what I have gone through now."

With this statement breathe deeply, and become, "being very OK at NOT being OK" with your situation. ***This practice makes you very grateful for your life situation all the time.***

The process described is linked to what I have been referring to in earlier chapters of the book. This is all part of 'the energy follows thoughts process' and teaches you to be a good energy banker. By allowing yourself to accept 'what is', neutralising your feelings, being aware of breathing and being in the present moment, you are actually allowing your energy to flow normally again. This simple and effective method allows you to have good health, and be in a calm state all the time when you are able to remember to be with your feelings. It makes you more conscious of 'what is' and you then become the architect of your life. You learn that you can have access to every part of your body and feelings. You will then start to accept and love yourself more and more and eventually, unconditionally.

You may like to make a few notes of your experiences and know that every experience that you apply this technique to, you will be able to make yourself calmer within a very short time. With practice you could make yourself quiet and calm within seconds. ***Just thinking "I am love" and being in your Heart Centre will make things change inside you, without going through the whole process.*** Again, to get to this stage you have to do this every day with all your unwanted emotions. When you are really good at this, all you do is note what is happening inside you, and you just breathe into it very quickly and say,

> "I am love, I am love", about 10 times, and then add, "I forgive whoever may have caused this feeling within me and I ask that my cells let go of the memories of the pain. I am also grateful for what I have got and I am blessed with abundance daily,"

Within seconds you are calm again. How quickly you get to this stage again depends on how quickly you get to know yourself. The sooner you are in touch with your feelings, the sooner you will start to clear any blockages that are within you from the past and the healthier you will become.

One of the ways to notice that your energy is being cleared is, when doing the process you start to yawn, or sigh, tears start to come out of your eyes, or your eyes start to blink quickly. You will also begin to feel more relaxed, you will feel this in the back and shoulders (most people get confused thinking that they are getting tired) these are signs that you should be experiencing. The more common one is yawning. The more you yawn when you are doing the breathing indicates that your blockage is clearing quickly.

LOVING YOURSELF MORE

When you begin to love yourself more, you will do what is necessary to be in good health. For example, the first thing you will start to look at is your diet. You will start to eat better and ensure you ingest less, or no chemicals at all. When I started off on my journey I was smoking 20 plus cigarettes per day and was also drinking quite excessively. I was eating junk food and lots of sweet things. What was being advertised on the TV, in newspapers or magazines I would purchase most of. As I began to accept and like myself more, I became more aware of what I was putting into my body. I started to read up on having a healthy body and I cut down on my intake of cigarettes and alcohol and eventually gave them all up. I now live on a simple and healthy diet (mainly fresh salads and fruits, no meat). I also believe in the saying that, "you are what you eat". Again there are thousands of good books being written about healthy eating and I am not going to tell you what to do. Be guided by your inner self and you will be guided to the right books to read about your diet. The more you begin to like yourself, the more you will invest the time in you.

The next thing that you will attend to is your physical body. Again this is a natural progression. When I was aware that my body was the most important thing that I had, I started to look after it. I started to exercise and took up chi gong, t'ai chi and yoga. I even joined a gym for several years. I didn't do all this in one go. In the many years that passed I started to learn different disciplines. ***What I did most consistently was walking.*** I read somewhere that the least one had to do was to walk for a mile in the morning and one mile in the evening and this I have done religiously for years. In the early days, I walked every day, morning and evening, and also drank at least 2 litres of water every day. I started to cut down on my intake of tea, coffee and soft drinks and eventually gave them all up. Today I only drink gallons of warm water.

When I mastered t'ai chi and chi gong, and then took up yoga, I spent my days rotating through the three disciplines throughout the week. Eventually I stopped doing t'ai chi and chi gong and just did yoga every day. I have been doing this for the past three years as I found yoga personally suited me better. I noticed that all the stretching helped me and that all my old aches and pains that I had when I was younger began to disappear. Today, the first thing, before I start on anything is to do the breathing exercises and then yoga. All this takes me about 90 minutes daily. I do this every day because I feel really good when I finish my exercises and this sets me up for the whole day.

I told you in the earlier chapters about us being timeless travellers. We have all the time in the world and we are really going nowhere. (Notice nowhere can also be in the NOW HERE) I love spending time with me and I now walk everywhere within 3 miles of my destinations. I try to use public transport more because it makes me walk and, as I am not in a hurry to get to anywhere now. I don't use the car much now; I use it only if the journey is over 7 miles and when it is difficult to get to my destination by public transport. Whatever your plans are, I would suggest that you do the following rigidly daily. ***Firstly, make sure that you drink a minimum of 2 litres of water***. This doesn't include teas, coffees, or other drinks. If you can train yourself to drink warm water daily, then you can replace all the hot drinks that you have. Your sense of taste becomes better and you don't need sweet or tasty drinks. ***Next, ensure that you walk at least two miles per day. I would suggest that if you can, walk in green areas, as this will also have a calming effect.*** This is the minimum that you have to do for yourself to start with and when you love yourself more, you will certainly find more time to be with yourself and do what is necessary. Again there are plenty of good books being written about exercising.

Loving yourself more means being able to be spend more time with yourself. You eat better, you take good care of your body, you listen to what you are saying and most importantly you learn to be more acceptable of yourself, and in doing this you become more acceptable of others. You become less of a judge, you allow others to express themselves and be themselves, you hold no judgements of others, and you just let them be. You love life for what it has to offer, and that is all there is and nothing else. ***Everything else that you concoct in your mind is an illusion. It is not true, for the truth is only in the now "Here Now".*** Being in the present moment makes everything perfect as it is and as you learn to stop thinking and just be quiet and observe, you learn that in the stillness you can have access to everything. In the stillness of all this you hear that tiny voice within you that is your intuition, it will guide you to newer levels of experiences and understanding.

HOW TO USE THIS NEW SKILL TO COPE WITH YOUR DAILY LIFE

Let's go back to an earlier chapter where I set out a typical day. Now, with your new skills, let me show you how you may approach the same situations. ***Nothing changes, only your attitude towards 'what is' has changed.***

A TYPICAL DAY: as described in earlier chapter

When we wake up in the morning our energy bank balance is high with credits of energy that were deposited in the night before by the universe, we are energy rich. We may get up, pull our curtains back and notice it is raining and perhaps make some comment about the weather, as we usually do, and we start to deplete our bank, (energy follows thought) we lose our energy to what we give our attention to so we are beginning to lose energy early in the day.

The truth of the matter is, it is raining, if we don't like rain because we have to walk in the weather, we put our judgement on to it and spend time giving it life in our minds, causing us to lose energy.

What we could do is, if the rain has caused us to be uncomfortable, we just start to notice where we feel this and breathe into it. We go through the process that I described earlier on and say to ourselves, "even though it is raining I love and approve of myself unconditionally". We do this until there are no judgements of the rain and you are OK with the rain. You may realise that the plants and trees need the rain and are happy for them because it has rained. So what happens is, you just accept the rain and get on with your life and maintain your energy level. (This is a very important part of the process that you go through from Step 1 to Step 4 in every situation, however, if the intensity level comes down quickly you don't have to do the whole process).

Then, when we turn on the radio or TV as we go about preparing for work, we hear bad news and we start to pay attention to it and more energy units are being used up.

We start to lose energy about what is happening and being reported by the radio or TV. The truth is something was reported that happened to someone in a situation. Your brain has gone into judgement of what has happened because you probably didn't like what you heard and you start thinking about it in the 'ifs', 'whys' and 'buts' and losing energy. The fact of the matter is you cannot do anything about it. You cannot change what has happened. You can't turn the clock back as if it didn't happen.

So, if you were triggered by what has happened, you take note of where you have these uncomfortable feelings in your body and you start to do the process and say to yourself, "even though this has happened and it has upset me and I can't do anything about it now, I love and approve of myself unconditionally," and do this until the intensity of the feelings have come down and you are back to normal.

We get our post and there is more bad news, we have overspent on our credit cards, more worry, and more energy being used up.

The fact is we have overspent; we can't do anything about it now so we just accept 'what is'. No use berating yourself or your partner for overspending. It doesn't change *anything. So if this causes you to go into judgment of self or others, all you do is breathe into the situation and say to yourself, "even though I have overspent and I am in trouble financially at the moment, I love and approve of myself unconditionally", and you repeat the process until you are calm again, and probably in the process you will realise that you have to set up some kind of budget to curb your spending. Now you are again retuning to your normal calm state. No energy is being lost unnecessarily and you are in control of what is happening to you.*

Carry on reading below and you will see that at every juncture where one used to lose energy, now one is able to breathe into the situation with the affirmation of, "even though this 'x' has happened, I love and approve of myself unconditionally", neutralising every situation and being in a calmer state. Of course this is the ideal situation and with practice you will get there in the end. You will of course forget during the day and do your usual patterns and use energy up, but this time you will lose less and the more aware you are of yourself, the less you will lose. Again with constant awareness and daily practice you will be a wealthy energy banker and be healthy. Of course this will take time.

****

As we go to work, whilst reading the paper either on the bus or train, or if we happen to travel to work by car listening to the radio, ...guess what? More bad news is being delivered to us. Or perhaps on our way we are worrying or berating ourselves about our overspending or perhaps wondering if the rain will stop by the time we get to work, or worrying about some other personal matter. This ***incessant chatting*** that goes on in our head never stops and is draining our energy constantly, and by the time we get to work, we are probably a little irritable because we start to feel stressed out, and we haven't even started work yet! My research has shown that

STRESS is an indication that the body is running low on energy. When we are low on energy, our body begins to tense up; we get irritable, our patience is virtually non-existence, we find fault with most things, we become intolerant, things begin to get too much and our muscles in our body become tighter without us realising it until we have pain. Everything becomes a big deal; even the smallest of incidents gets over exaggerated. Everything seems to get out of hand. ***Eventually we get pains throughout the body as we tense more***. These pains could end up in any part of your body, but the most common areas are in your stomach region, chest and back areas. In some cases the knees and joints. This is only an indication that we are running low on energy and that there is also an energy blockage in the body's system. When you get tensed, energy doesn't flow as easily as if you were relaxed, hence the blockage. Blockage means that energy is not flowing. Just like a drainpipe that is clogged up with garbage, causing a blockage.

All during the day we keep losing more energy. Our chatterbox doesn't stop talking in our brain and we get even more tired. Most of us don't take any notice of how we feel, as we haven't been trained to. We carry on regardless of what is happening inside us thinking this is how life is. Nobody told us any different. ***The sad part of it all is, through our ignorance we eventually become ill because we have depleted our energy system. The good news is, it takes us many years before the disease sets in. Now that you have this material you can do something about it before your illness becomes degenerative.***

****

Now, just to recap this lesson.

- **Step 1: Basic training. Be aware of your feelings, and pay attention to them.**
- **Step 2: Awareness training. Pay attention to your feelings wherever they are.**
- **Step 3: The forgiveness and letting go technique. Forgive yourself and others that may have caused you this pain.**
- **Step 4: Being Grateful technique. Be Grateful for what you have.**

Please ensure that you know this chapter well and I would suggest that you read this chapter over and over until you are able to do the process without having to refer back to the book. ***You need to memorise this for maximum benefit.***

When you have learnt to know the differences in your feelings, I want you to go back to your notes and re-read what you have written in the pages where you have had unpleasant memories from the past. These are the notes I asked you to make in the earlier chapters. I want you to do the process with the uncomfortable situations from your past and notice how the situation affects you now. It shouldn't have any affect on you after doing the process and if it has, you have to repeat the process over and over until the intensity levels come down. Eventually, what you will be left with is a sense of what happened, 'what is', with no judgements about the situation and you will not have an emotional attachment to it. It is like you are watching a movie but are not in the actual movie, if you know what I mean.

Make the time as soon as possible to record all the incidents that have happened to you in the past that had an adverse effect on you in your journal. These could be incidents where you were bullied at school, your teachers or friends made fun of you, scolding you had from your parents, try listing every painful experience that you can remember. This is going to take a while. If you have only about 50 experiences, then I suggest that you start to get in touch with your feelings. Probably the experiences that you have chosen to forget were experiences that were so bad that you chose to never remember them. The body is very clever at protecting itself and causes us to forget, to protect ourselves from more pain. In this exercise you should have hundreds of experiences to list.

Make the time for yourself to go through your journal and do the process with each incident that has caused you pain. Go through each one until the intensity levels come down. Remember before you start each exercise first note the intensity levels. There is no rush to get this all done in one go but I would suggest that you start to make time to clear your past. The more you do the process, the better you will be at clearing your past and soon you will be able to clear your patterns within minutes when they occur, and your past will not be able to haunt you anymore. You will rid yourself of your emotional baggage and be rid of all those negative feelings and begin to heal. All those old aches and pains in your body will begin to disappear. You are getting to know yourself better and are beginning to heal daily.

An Alternative Method "Emotional Freedom Technique"

"Argue for your limitations and they are yours.
Argue for your possibilities and they are yours as well"
Various authors

AN ALTERNATIVE METHOD

I hope that you have mastered the previous chapter because in this chapter I am going to share with you an alternative method that is equally effective in my opinion. When you learn to apply these two methods together the problems from your past will definitely be erased. The memories will still be there but there will be no emotional charges to them. It will all seem like a movie with no special effects.

Gary Craig, a Stanford graduate and an engineer by profession with no medical background, developed this technique known as **"Emotional Freedom Technique"**. I came across Gary's technique some years back, researched into it and found that there are many similarities with Chi Integration. I find EFT equally powerful and have no hesitation in recommending it. I am going to share with you a simplified and modified version of what Gary recommends and by applying this, either separately or jointly, to the techniques that I have introduced to you in the previous chapter you will be able to assist yourself in any situation. When you combine the two, you just breathe deeply and tap at the same time saying the affirmations.

EFT is based on the premise that the body's energy system is linked to energy circuits, or meridians, that run throughout the body. The state of these meridians is directly affected by our emotional and physical health. By analogy, think of the meridians as rivers. Upsets in emotional or physical health lead to the equivalent of blockages or overflows in the rivers. By correcting the meridians i.e. restoring the body's energy status, the emotional/physical disorder is corrected.

This is done by tapping with fingers on certain acupunctures points on the face, torso and hand, while "tuning in" to the problem in your mind. Through these points we can access important meridians of the body and by tapping on them, excessive negative emotional energy is released. The difference between the process recommended in the last chapter and EFT is, with EFT you tap on the recommended acupuncture points and with the breathing process you breathe in the area where you have the feelings and by breathing to those areas it clears the blockages and allows the energy to circulate through the meridian system. The breath, when done consciously, pushes energy through the meridian systems and clears it of any blockages.

TAPPING TECHNIQUE (Emotional Freedom Technique)

- Step 1. Name the problem. Let's assume that you feel tightness in your chest and you find it difficult to breathe because you may be afraid.
- Step 2. Take your intensity level reading. The number 10 will indicate that you are very fearful and difficulty breathing and zero representing being very calm and relaxed. Your reading should be between 1 and 10. Again if you are not sure what it is, just guess.
- Step 3. Do the set up phrase. "Even though I have this problem, this tightness in my chest, and I find it difficult to breathe because I am afraid, I love and accept myself unconditionally", say it three times. Or you can just say, "Even though I have this problem, I love and accept myself unconditionally", again you say it three times. Whilst you are saying

this you rub your "Sore Point" with all your fingers. This point is on the left-hand side of your breast just one inch about your nipple. If you press this point you will find that it hurts. Don't worry if you can't find this point, by just rubbing this area with your fingers you are accessing it. When you get to know your body better you will recognise the sore point.

- Step 4. Repeat the Set Up Phrase again three times but this time you are tapping your Karate Chop Point. This point in on the side of your hand, roughly in line with your lifeline. (If you watch Martial Arts and see how they use their hands to "chop" breaking up bricks or slates or blocks of wood that is the part you are going to tap on). It doesn't matter which hand you tap on or which side of your body you tap. When you are tapping your points, you do it lightly.

There are nine major points to tap once you have done your set up phrases on your sore point and karate chop point. You tap on these nine points about 7 times and repeat a shortened version of your set up phrase. In this instance you will just say "this problem" which is connected to your set up phrase. When you are saying "this problem", and breathing deeply you tap on the next nine points.

1. The first point you tap will be on your crown, top of your head. You use all five fingers to tap. Repeating the shortened version phrase and tap about seven times lightly on the crown. You could use either hand or both hands.

2. The second point is on the eyebrow, this is where the bone behind your eyebrow turns into the bridge of your nose. I know that your fingers will cover over it, just pull in your fingers and make them a smaller group. You are tapping on the bone on the socket of the inner eye.

3. Next is the corner of the eye. Again on the bone in the corner of your eye.

4. The next point is under the eye. On the bone just below your eye, in line with your pupil if you look straight ahead.

5. Next is under the nose, this is the point between your nose and your upper lip.

6. Under The Mouth, tap in the indentation between your chin and your lower lip.

7. Next is the Collarbone. Tap in the angle formed by your collarbone and the breastbone.

8. Next point is under the Arm. Tap in line with the nipple on the side of the body, for ladies, where the side of your bra strap is.

9. Last point is under your nipple about 2 inches below. For women it is just below the breast.

After you have done the nine points, take a deep breath and take an intensity count. Again you will start to notice something happening inside of your body. You repeat the above exercises until your intensity level comes down to zero, or as close as possible. Keep tapping until you feel relaxed. This may take a few minutes. After this, do the forgiving and letting go technique, and ending with the gratitude technique given in the last chapter.

Before you read any further please make sure that you know the two techniques thoroughly.

HOW TO USE YOUR NEW SKILLS DAILY

Now that you have these techniques, how are you going to deal with your daily challenges? When do you use them? The answer is, you use them all the time on everything. Yes, everything. You tap and breathe into every situation that causes you an upset.

What do you think that upsets you most of the time? When your expectations are not met.

This is a very simple and powerful statement. Yes, every time you get upset, it is because something doesn't go according to your plans and you start to judge the situation. In most cases we get disappointed and would like to blame someone for something that hasn't gone according to our plans. We blame others or ourselves. Our inability to accept "change" causes us to lose energy. To overcome this you simply learn to let go of your expectations. Easier said then done. This is going to be difficult, as we all don't like change. It will take you a while to be able to let go of your expectations and accept "what is". First of all you have to be aware that you are upset and are in judgement, and by noticing that you are in this situation you are able to do something about it. The majority of people are not aware and just carry on as normal and lose their energy daily and eventually becoming ill. When you become aware, you know how to pay attention to what is happening in your body and perform the processes described earlier. The faster you are able to connect to your upset feelings, the quicker you will be able to learn to let go of your expectations and accept 'what is'.

When your expectation is not met, you normally go into judgement and blame, and the emotional pain will drain your life force, your energy bank. Now that you have your new skills you are able to control what is happening inside you and also the dialogue that goes on in your mind. ***The dialogue is either attacking someone or defending someone. It is either in the future or the past, never in the present moment***. This incessant talking goes on and on and if you don't correct it, you lose too much energy. The mere fact that you are aware of what is happening within you means that you are able to correct it and bring yourself to the present, the now.

Describe in your 'set up' phrases 'what is'

For example: let's suppose your partner promised to do something important for you and they forgot to do it. Of course you will be upset or may be angry. Your set up phrase will be, "Even though I am angry at my partner for forgetting to do that important thing for me, I love and accept myself unconditionally." Check your intensity charge and do either of the processes or both together to bring the intensity levels down. This will take you a few minutes and then you can carry on as normal without holding a grudge against your partner. You are able to accept the situation that your partner forgot to do something for you. Your energy is flowing freely again.

Or your boss shouts at you because you have not done your job correctly, according to him, and you are upset about being shouted at. Your set up phrase would be, "Even though my boss shouts at me and I think he is unreasonable, I still love and approve of myself unconditionally."

Go through the process until the intensity level comes down and you are accepting of your boss's action. You are OK with him having shouted at you and have accepted his actions; perhaps he could have been right in having shouted at you or maybe he was just stressed out because of his deadlines or maybe it was your fault anyway, maybe your work wasn't up to standard in that instance and the action taken by your boss was acceptable. When you start to neutralise your feelings, you begin to see different points of view, you are not fixed like before where you would have gone into victim mode or judging your boss.

The more options you allow yourself to look at, the more flexible you will become. You start to accept and understand other people's points of view. There will come a time when you will understand that everybody is right from his or her perspective and learn to respect everyone's view, even if you disagree. You allow others to be who they want to be and accept them for not behaving to your expectations.

Express your true feelings in the set up phrases. If you are angry say you are angry, if you are fearful, say you are fearful. The rule is, whatever you feel you say. "Even though I feel "X" (X being any of your emotions or actions), I love and approve of myself unconditionally." Even if you hate yourself you could say, "Even though I hate myself for having done this, I love and approve of myself unconditionally."

WHERE DO YOU DO YOUR PROCESSING?

You do your processing whenever you are upset. For example, if your boss shouts at you and you are upset, and as you are standing in front of him and recognizing how you feel, you could say the set up phrases quietly in your mind and start to breathe into that part of your body that feels uncomfortable, deeply and slowly. Check your intensity count and keep repeating the process until the count comes down. The mere fact that you started to do something about it will help you. Normally when something like this happens, we react and go straight into judgement and the incessant, chatterbox brain starts. We either start to justify our position by either attacking or defending our actions, and if we do nothing about it, we will be thinking about the situation repeatedly over and over in our brains and depleting our energy bank.

If it is not possible for you to do the processing there and then, you could excuse yourself and go somewhere quiet and do the breathing and tapping simultaneously until your intensity level comes down. All this new training is going to test you. ***Sometimes we refuse to do the breathing and tapping because we want to be right and want to be angry***. I know that feeling well, as there have been many times I didn't want to shift as my Ego got the better of me and guess who suffered in the long run? Me! I ended up being bad tempered and stressed out. I have learnt from bitter experiences not to fight change if I wanted to be in harmony with my environment and maintain good health. I know for definite that your Ego will affect you the same way mine did, in trying to stop me to changing, as ***the Ego does not like change. It likes to be in control***. This is where the battle will be and sometimes we just plain forget to do the process as the Ego has taken over completely and we revert back to our old ways. This will not last for long I assure you, if you keep reminding yourself that you want to go forward in your development, re-reading this material and other similar books will keep you focused. You may take one step forward and half a step back and sometimes two steps forward and two steps back but forward you will surely go. It is not a steep climb up the mountain; you will go up and down the valleys to get to the peak. This is how the journey will be for all of us. I know that if you persist and keep the persistence up, you will be in control in the end and contain your energy losses.

USE THE PROCESS FOR EVERY SITUATION

In my marketing brochures I list the following painful emotions that I teach people how to release themselves from but really it can be used for every uncomfortable situation.

My brochure states, "Release yourself from"

- Addictions
- Anger
- Anxiety, Depression & Stress
- Blocked Grief
- Lack of Self Confidence.
- Emotional Traumas
- Exam Nerves
- Fear of Fear
- Fear of Flying & Heights
- Health Problems
- Panic Attacks
- Phobias
- Public Speaking
- Relationship Issues
- Relief of Physical Pain
- Sexual Abuse Issues
- Weight & Eating Disorders

There are seventeen examples above and I am going to go through with you some of them so that you may begin to have a solid foundation and understanding of doing the "process" and learning how you can be totally comfortable being uncomfortable. ***It's OK NOT to be OK.***

ADDICTIONS

Back in 1997 when I was doing voluntary work at a Drug Centre in Southall, Middlesex, I tried and tested the techniques and had a very good success rate. During the three years that I was there, I improved and modified the "process" and with the feedback and results I received from the clients, I now have a proven system achieving a very high level of success. The problem with drugs is that they have physical withdrawal systems and it is more difficult for the addicts to rid themselves of the habit because they get physical withdrawal systems like being sick or cramps in the stomach when they don't take the drug. In instances like this the addict has to be slowly weaned off over a period of time by reducing the dosage as time goes on. The "process" will however stop the cravings but not the sickness; and the process will also reduce the intensity of pain of the cramps in the stomach making it more bearable when in cold turkey.

With clients that are addicted to cigarettes, every time that they crave the nicotine I ask them to hold the cigarette in their hands, look at it, then smell it under their nose and bring their intensity of craving to ten, at this point they feel that they must smoke the cigarette.

When the intensity level goes to ten and the craving is at its highest, I ask them where they have this urge in their body and most say somewhere in the solar plexus area. Others say it is in their head, some say that their heart rate is racing. I ask them to concentrate on where this feeling is and start the "process". In this instance, we would do the quick breathing, then pay attention to the cravings and start to breathe long breaths and say the following, "Even though I have this craving for this cigarette and I really need to smoke to satisfy my needs, I deeply accept and love myself unconditionally." They may also add, "Even though I am weak and am controlled by this cigarette, I love and approve of myself unconditionally." As you get good at this, you become more creative with your wordings and phrases. You could really start to disapprove of yourself for wanting the cigarette and in the "process" you will always end by saying, "I love and approve of myself unconditionally."

The clients keep repeating the statement and breathing deeply until the craving goes down to zero. When the craving has dispersed, there is no urge or need for the cigarette. When they are in the "forgiving process" they sometimes have insights as to why and what started them smoking. They can identify the cause of it. This usually goes back to something that happened in the past, when smoking was either connected to reducing stress or to bring some form of comfort. When they address the "cause" of it, the symptoms disappears and there is no need for cigarettes or any other drug that they are addicted to. They work through the "cause" in the same way with the "process". An example would be, "Even though when I failed my GCSE back in the past and that caused me to smoke when I was only 15 years old, I love and approve of myself unconditionally."

When you combine the breathing with the EFT start with the set up phrase. Repeat the set up phrase, breathe deeply and rub the sore point, then proceed to tap several times on the karate chop point. Then, keep tapping on all points, as recommended earlier on in the chapter on EFT, and maintain and keep doing the deep breathing at the same time and saying the affirmation until the craving for the nicotine goes right down. The tapping and verbalisation carries on until the craving completely disappears.

When you have completed the above, you have to retest the situation. You have to repeat the experiment again and find out what the intensity level is when you put the cigarette under the nose and find out if there is still a craving for the cigarette. If there is, check the intensity level again and repeat the process again and keep retesting until there is no more craving when you retest.

Once this is mastered, you are in control as every time the craving comes up you just repeat the "process" until the craving goes and eventually there are no more cravings and you have rid yourself of this dreadful, smelly habit, saving thousands of pounds being a non-smoker, not forgetting the fact that you will also be much healthier.

The above process can also be applied to any other type of addiction. If you overeat, make the same approach when your cravings are for food and you say, "Even though I have this craving for "x" and I am weak and cannot resist "x", I love and approve of myself unconditionally."

I personally have a real weakness for cashew nuts and find them irresistible. So when I am faced with the nuts, I have them in front of me and I do the process saying, "Even though I have this desire for these nuts and I am weak as it controls me, I love and approve myself unconditionally." I do the breathing and also the tapping at the same time until the craving disappears. Now, every time I have the desire I have the nuts in front of me and I just take a deep breath and breathe deeply for a few rounds and the nuts have no effect on me.

You can use the same technique with addictions to food. If you want to lose weight, all you have to do is to face all your desires in wanting whatever food has control over you and do the process.

If you are a "spendaholic" and can't resist spending, again all you have to do is walk into the shop, stand in front of what you want to buy and say to yourself, "Even though I want to purchase "x" so baldy as it will make me feel good, I love and accept myself unconditionally," you say this and breathe and tap until the urge goes and then you just walk away. You keep doing this until you are in control. Usually, by the time you get to the forgiving process in your deep breathing you will realise your need to buy is probably to comfort yourself. Research has proven that we do things to comfort ourselves most of the time as we do not love and approve of ourselves enough. When you start to like and love yourself more, your needs for external things diminish and you will only then buy what is required. Fashion will be a thing of the past, as you will like yourself in whatever you wear.

You apply the process to all type of behaviour patterns that controls you. Gambling, overeating, overspending, over drinking, overworking, excessive sexual desires, anything that you overindulge in and that takes most of your attention and controls you.

All addictions are a cry for attention/help; they help us escape from our pain from our past and present and we keep repeating them not realising that our pain from the past is so powerful, When we can address the emotional issues, the addictions will cease. Again, through the forgiving and gratitude process, you will be able to access your emotional issues and start to forgive yourself and others that have caused you to be the way you are.

ANGER, ANXIETY, DEPRESSION, STRESS AND BLOCK GRIEF

Anger, anxiety, depression, stress and block grief can all be treated in the same way as the addiction approach. With Anger, all you say to yourself, "Even though I am angry with "x" because of……………., I love and accept myself unconditionally." You can do the breathing and tapping technique together or separately to bring the intensity level down until you have neutralised it.

In all the set up statements that you use you will use the words and sentences that are applicable to your uncomfortable feelings. So if you are stressed, you would say, "Even though I am stressed at this situation, I accept and love myself unconditionally".

If you have a phobia about snakes or spiders or fear of dogs, again all you have to do is to use the set up, "Even though I have a phobia of "x" and it really scares the hell out of me, I love and accept myself unconditionally." I personally had a phobia of snakes, and every time I noticed a picture of a snake on TV or read about it I would do the process and through persistence I am now not phobic of snakes anymore. Another phobia I had was that I found it difficult to watch any operations on the human body on TV. The cutting of the organs and sight of blood would make me squeamish and I had to cover my eyes and peep through the gaps in my fingers. Since I have applied the process, every time I see a programme the feelings of squeamishness disappear, and now I am able to watch any medical programme or operations, as I am not affected.

PAIN CONTROL

The "process" is very powerful for pain control. I use it for pains in my body or headaches. I locate where the pain is and rate the intensity and start the process. The pain sometimes travels to different parts of the body, I then "chase the pain" and eventually when I track the pain to a certain point and it doesn't travel around anymore, the pain would reduce or disappears. I had an old injury on my left shoulder due to a sports injury. The doctors diagnosed it as "frozen shoulder" and I must have had it for over 40 years and during the course of the 40 years I had different treatments and painkillers. The treatments were ineffective. The intensity of the pain would come down to about a '4' and I had to live with it for most of the time. Since becoming a healer and doing the process on myself I have managed to bring the intensity down to about a '1'and sometimes it is zero.

I managed to control the pain in my shoulder, but it was weak due to the lack of movement over the years. I tried weights at the gym but I couldn't lift much weight and it was painful and I was advised by the trainers at the club to cease doing weights. It was when I started Yoga on a regular basis that my shoulder and left arm started to be stronger and I now have 95% mobility in the injured shoulder. Through my research I also know that the bones are the most difficult parts of the body to heal and for the cells in the bones to regenerate completely it will take seven years. I have done 3 years of yoga and already I have felt a great improvement, and am looking forward to the next few years to be totally pain free and have a strong shoulder and arm.

I have taught the process to clients with the following physical problems: cramps in the stomach, constipation, muscular aches and pains, arthritis in joints and fingers, headaches, migraines, backaches, and rashes. All have reported improvements after they applied the process. In some difficult degenerative cases with constant persistence they found that they could eventually control the pain. I personally have used it for toothaches and found that it reduces the pain. Here you have your own built-in painkiller. Basically, what you are doing is really getting in touch with your body parts. Your body is part of you and is not separate from you. The sooner you realise this, the sooner you will be able to do wonders and communicate with the cells in your body. When you have more success with the process and understand that your cells are all part of you, you will then speak to that part of your body and eventually through insights, you will be able to hand the power to your body to take care of what is wrong with you. All this comes with practice, and the more you do, the more you will understand about your body. Your body is able to communicate with you when you learn to be still and quiet.

TRY THE PROCESS ON EVERYTHING

Whatever the problem is, please, use the 'process', after all, what do you have to lose? All you have to do is to make sure that the set up wording is correct. How do you know what is the correct wording is? Just use the words that describe your situation at the time.

- For example, if you were afraid of public speaking, your set up would be, "Even though I am afraid of public speaking I love and accept myself unconditionally."

- If you were afraid of flying, "Even though I am afraid of flying because, whatever the reason is............, I love and accept myself unconditionally."
- With emotional traumas just describe what happened, "Even though this terrible situation happened to me when I was young (be specific of situation and the age you were and try to be as close to it as you remember) and I cannot forgive whoever, I love and approve of myself unconditionally".

With any situation where you have started with the set up phrase and have done the intensity count, begin the process of deep breathing and tapping until the intensity count comes down. Sometimes you may have instant relief and sometimes it will take you longer, like an hour and other times more. Every situation that you encounter will be different; after you have done this for a while you will understand how it works. In the beginning you will do things very mechanically and you will find that you will get results and with practice you will get better at it. ***The chaos does not change in your world. What changes is your perception.*** This is what makes you, ***"being OK at NOT being OK."*** Life goes on irrespective of what is happening to you in your life, and the only way forward is to be non-judgemental of 'what is'. Always report it as you see it.................'what is'.

Case Study Using "Breathing Method"

CASE STUDY: Lynn (using the breathing technique only)

Learning to ask questions when doing " the process"

Asking questions when we are doing the process helps get us to the cause of our initial problem quicker, and helps us shift our perceptions. It is like peeling an onion. There are many levels that we may have to go through to get to the real/root cause. Remember that our caretakers mainly installed into us everything that we have experienced in the past. Let me give you an example: The name of the client has been changed for obvious reasons. Let's call her Lynn.

Lynn, a 47-year-old woman married for 20 years with 3 children aged 19, 16 and 3, came to me with many problems and she didn't know where or how to begin to tell me about her many problems. She was unhappy, depressed, tired all the time and not pleased with her husband. She told me she thought she wasn't a good mother/person because she couldn't protect her children from the mental abuse her husband was inflicting on them and herself. Whilst she could cope with him being nasty to her, she also felt the pain her children were going through when her husband picked on them. From what Lynn told me I could only assume that she was obviously also a very emphatic person. As she didn't know where to start with her problems, I thought I would just ask a few questions to see where it took us. I asked her about her husband's behaviour and wanted to know how she considered him to be a nasty and unreasonable person.

Me: Lynn, tell me, what is it that your husband does that makes you unhappy?

Lynn: He's very uncaring.

Me: Uncaring? How is he uncaring and when is he uncaring?

Lynn: Recently, my eldest son was in hospital and had to undergo an operation, it wasn't a really big operation or dangerous, but my husband didn't care and this made me angry with him.

Me: So, you are unhappy with your husband because your son was undergoing an operation at the hospital and you assumed that he wasn't caring. Is that correct?

Lynn: Yes.

Me: When you are talking to me about the incident now, how unhappy are you, if 10 being very unhappy and zero being calm where are you now?

Lynn: I would say it's about an 8.

Me: Do you feel any pains, either emotional or physical in your body when you are unhappy about this situation? Perhaps like tightness in your chest or churning in your stomach?

Lynn: No, I don't feel any of those things, but I feel that I can't breathe deeply and yes, there is tightness around my chest area.

We started to do the process. I told her what to do and she paid attention to her chest area where the pain intensity was 8. She was with that part of her body for a few seconds, and I instructed her to breathe quickly for 20 seconds in and out.

Me: How are you feeling now?

Lynn: A little better

Me: What do you think your intensity level is now?

Lynn: About a 6.

Me: How do you know that you are a 6?

Lynn: Well, my chest seems looser and I'm a little more relaxed.

Me: Now I want you to take a few long breaths for a few minutes, the breaths must be 3-5 seconds in and the same for the out breath, and when you are doing the breathing, I want you to say to yourself, or in your mind, "Even though my husband is uncaring and I have this pain in my chest, I love and approve of myself." Repeat this while you are breathing in and out.

Lynn tried this for a few breaths and said that she wasn't feeling comfortable with saying that she loves and approves of herself.

Me: You don't feel good about saying that you love and approve of yourself? Why?

Lynn: It doesn't feel right.

Me: OK, let's change it to, "Even though my husband is uncaring and I have this pain in my chest, I am willing to accept and like myself." Try this new statement and let me know if you are OK with it?

Lynn did the new affirmation and said that she was OK with it. I then instructed her to carry on with the deep breathing for about 1 minute.

Me: What is happening within you now?

Lynn: Feels a little lighter.

Me: I want you to change the statement to, "Even though my husband is uncaring and I feel lighter, I like and approve of myself."

She did it and carried on for a while doing the breathing and repeating the new affirmation.

Me: What is happening and how do you feel now Lynn?

Lynn: I'm not so unhappy with him now and I think hospitals are an uncaring and scary place.

Me: That's good that you aren't so unhappy with him, tell me, how do you know that hospitals are an uncaring place and how do you know that?

Lynn: When I was a young girl, I was in hospital and it wasn't a nice place, I didn't like it.

Me: How old were you when you were in hospital?

Lynn: I think I was about 6 years old.

Me: Do you know why you were in hospital?

Lynn: My mum told me that I was always sick and she had to put me into hospital.

Me: How long were you in hospital, Lynn, when you were a little girl?

Lynn: I don't know but it seems that I was always going in and out of hospital and always being left alone as my mother had to go home and leave me there.

Me: Now that we are talking about you being a child in hospital at 6 years old, what are you feeling inside you? (***Notice that the emphasis from being unhappy with the husband has shifted and moved to the hospital being an uncaring and scary place, layers of the onions being removed***)

Lynn: About a 10.

Me: Are you really scared thinking about it, and is it a ten?

Lynn: Yes.

Me: Are you feeling anything in your body with this 10?

Lynn: I feel tightness in my heart area.

Me: I want you to pay attention to that area for a while and then place your palm on your heart chakra (area around the heart) and breathe quickly for a few seconds.

She did as she was instructed.

Me: Lynn, when you are feeling a little more comfortable, start to breathe longer breaths and say to yourself, "Even though the hospital is an uncaring and scary place and I have tightness in my heart area, I accept myself unconditionally." Keep saying this for a minute while you are breathing in and out with long breaths.

Lynn did as she was instructed.

Me: What is happening in your body now and what is the intensity count now?

Lynn: I feel the same, but I'm now very angry with my mother for leaving me in the hospital. I am angry with her for not being with me. (Again we are shifting from hospital to her mother now)

Me: Repeat after me Lynn whilst you are breathing in long and out breathes. "Even though my mother left me alone in the hospital and I am very angry with her for doing that to me when I was so young, I deeply accept myself unconditionally." I want you to breathe in and out slowly, repeating this affirmation for about a minute or so, or until the count comes down.

Lynn did as she was told and said the affirmation and breathed. I let her do this for a few minutes and I was watching her for a while.

Me: Lynn, when you feel calmer you may stop and be with your new feelings.

Lynn: I feel much calmer, but I'm still angry at my mother for leaving me there and not being with me. She shouldn't have left me there on my own.

Me: Lynn, are you unhappy with your husband now? (I changed the subject and asked her about her husband, which was what we started with)

Lynn: No, I am not unhappy with him now, I am angry with my mother.

Me: What is the intensity?

Lynn: About a 6.

Me: Ok, I want you to say this now, and keep the long breathing in/out and try to make it longer if possible, let's say 5 seconds for in, and five for out. I want you to say, ***"Even though I am still angry with my mother for leaving me in hospital, and I forgive myself for being angry with her, I still accept myself unconditionally."*** (I am trying to introduce the forgiveness and letting go process)

Lynn did as instructed and breathed longer in and out with the new affirmation for a few minutes and seemed a little more relaxed.

Me: What is happening now, Lynn?

Lynn: I'm not angry with my mum now as I think she was doing her best for me then, but she shouldn't have left me alone as it was very scary for a little six-year-old.

Me: Lynn, keep breathing your long breaths and say, "Even though my mother should not have left the six-year-old child to be on her own, I forgive her as I think she was doing the best she could at the time. I also ask the memory in my cells to let go of the pain the six-year-old child was going through, and I love and accept myself." (Notice that I have now introduced the forgiveness and the letting go process)

Lynn did as she was told and after a few seconds, I asked her what was happening, she replied that she felt much better.

Me: Lynn, I want you to sit quietly and imagine bringing white light down into you and pour light all over you while you are breathing in and out. I want you to quietly say to yourself in your mind, "Even though I had this experience I am grateful for what I experienced and that I could have been worse off. I also know that there were other children who were much worse off than me and that my mother really did try her best but because she had to go to work, look after my brother and father as well, she did her best by putting me in hospital and it was the best care available at the time. I am glad that she did the best for me and I forgive her and myself and accept and love myself unconditionally."

(I know that this is rather a long statement, so I asked her to recall this part as best as she could as I had already planted the seeds for her in helping her with the statement. Before I asked her to say it I asked Lynn how she felt about the statement that I helped construct for her and she said that it sounded fine and was comfortable with it. This is important for if she didn't feel comfortable, it would not be true to her in her reality.

Lynn did this part of the exercise and I left her to be on her own for a few minutes before I asked her how she was feeling again.

Lynn: I'm really OK about that incident in the hospital and I realise that my mother did the best for me.

Me: Are you unhappy with your husband now for neglecting or being uncaring about your son being in hospital? (RETESTING)

Lynn: No I'm not, I suppose I felt my son's pain being in hospital and I imagined that he would be scared and because my husband didn't make a fuss about his operation, I assumed that he didn't care and was uncaring. I must have associated the little girl (myself when I was six years old) and her mother with my husband and son and I was angry with him like I was angry with my mother. I now realise that hospitals are not scary places and that it is a caring place where they help people heal.

Me: Now thinking back, I want you to tell me how you feel now about the whole thing? (RETESTING AGAIN)

Lynn: I feel very calm and I'm not angry with my husband, I realise that now. I feel good having done all that breathing and I must go back and apologise to my husband.

QUESTIONS TO ASK YOURSELF WHEN DOING THE PROCESS

I know that I will not be able to guide you through asking the questions when you are doing the process on your own. I have given you examples of what to ask yourself when you are doing the process. Even if you are not sure of what to ask to start with, just doing the breathing and the affirmation on what you are feeling at the time will bring the intensity count down. When you learn to ask leading questions, you will move faster through the pain and get to the core issues. The most important question to ask yourself is, ***"Who taught me this? Who said this to me and where did I learn it from?"*** and if you are not sure, you can say, "Even though I do not know who did this to me or taught this to me, I love and accept myself unconditionally."

When you are doing the breathing and saying the affirmation to yourself, you will be amazed at what new information comes from the past that you weren't aware of before you started. You will begin to see some of the clarity of your situation with less intensity and they will not seem to be such a big deal. I always breathe and close my eyes when I am doing the process and allow my mind to be still. During the stillness, I have a sense of what happened then, and I seem to have a different perception of what really did happen. Then, when I ask the questions, "Where did I learn this?" Or, "who did this to me", I have a different understanding of the situation, which is most beneficial to me.

There are many incidents where you don't have to go through the whole process as described above. Just working with the awareness technique, breathing and doing the affirmation on how you feel at the time and accepting who you are will bring the intensity levels down immediately.

The example that I gave about Lynn was a complex one done in one session of 60 minutes. When she had further sessions with me, she confirmed that her husband was also very similar to her mother, who was always criticising her and putting her down. We also had to deal with her self-esteem and, when we finished with her self-esteem in the next session, she also said that her husband had been unfaithful to her a few years before. She was really angry with him and hadn't forgiven him and she really wanted to punish him and wasn't able to forgive him.

To lash out at him and try to punish him she found faults with him for everything he did. She was also a very critical woman and guess who she learned this from? Her mother criticised her most of the time when she was a child and Lynn grew up trying to be a perfectionist to please her mother. Every small incident became a big deal. The incident about the hospital with her husband being uncaring was a minor incident, but in her mind it was a big deal. Her real anger was about him being unfaithful to her and she also felt betrayed. Just like she felt betrayed when she was in hospital when she was a girl. In the many sessions that followed we dealt with the betrayal and abandonment issues.

Case Study "Using Tapping Method"

CASE STUDY: Rose (using the tapping technique).

Rose (not her real name) was a 50 years old, married with two grown up children, who had left home, and had a husband who recently had a heart attack. Rose came to see me with problems of either being very high i.e. happy, or being very low i.e. sad/depressed. She informed me that she had been like this most of her life and emphasised that she was a very caring person. She said she was a good mother and wife and would do anything for her family's happiness. (Remember that what is being related to me is the other person's perception of how they see their reality).

Me: Rose, tell me, what are your real problems and fears?

Rose: I have highs and lows, when I'm happy, I'm very happy and when I'm sad, I get fearful that something bad is going to happen to me.

Me: How often do you get highs and lows, do you have more highs or more lows?

Rose: I think I have more lows and I don't like it when I'm low. I always think that something bad is going to happen to me. Also when I'm feeling low I get very tired. (This tells me that her monkey brain is working overtime and she is not present, she is thinking about her problems and fear all the time and losing energy)

Me: What do you mean, something bad is always going to happen to you when you are low?

Rose: When things are going well for me. I just think that this can't last and something is going to happen. Then I start to fear that something bad is going to happen to me. I feel that God is punishing me when something goes wrong.

This to me is interesting that she has this belief that if something is not going right for her, she is bad and God is going to punish her. Obviously this idea must have been planted in her mind during early childhood and as a grown woman she still believes this.

I decided that I would address this part of her problems first before taking things further and I explained to her about the EFT tapping technique. I told her to follow me and repeat after me what I was going to say. Before we started, I asked her to remember a time when things started to go wrong recently.

Me: Rose, I want you to go back to a time recently where you had this feeling that something would go wrong.

Rose: It was a couple of months ago in the summer when I was on holiday.

Me: Tell me what happened.

Rose: My husband had a heart attack and it ruined our holiday.

Me: Talking about this incident, how do you feel now?

Rose: I'm angry that my husband became ill and the holiday was ruined and we spent so much money.

Me: If 10 is you being very angry and zero being calm, where are you when you talk about the holiday now?

Rose: I think it's an 8.

Me: How do you know it's an 8?

Rose: Well, it feels like it and my heart is pounding a little faster, and when that happens, I know that I am getting stressed out.

Me: Are you able to breathe freely now Rose?

Rose: I think so, but I think I could breathe more deeply.

Me: Just follow me and repeat after me Rose (I was rubbing my sore spot and repeated the affirmation three times), "Even though it is difficult to have full breath, it is safe to breathe and I accept myself unconditionally."

Then we tapped on the side of the hand, on the karate chop, tapping about 7 times and repeating the affirmation three times. After that we went through all the points starting on top of the head and I changed the affirmation to, "It is safe to breathe". We did the tapping on the points for about 7 taps on each point and said the affirmation 3 times at each point.

Rose followed my instructions and when we finished the sequence I said.

Me: Rose, I want you to take a deep breath and let me know if it is easier to breathe now compared to earlier on.

Rose took a few deep breaths and replied.

Rose: I feel much easier in my chest now.

Me: OK Rose, I want you to tell me the intensity of your emotions when you think of the holiday now.

Rose: It's still about the same.

Me: Is your heart still pounding fast?

Rose: Yes.

Me: Follow me and also repeat what I am saying.

Rubbing the sore spot and repeating, "Even though my heart is pounding faster, and my holiday was ruined because my husband had a heart attack, I accept myself unconditionally." I repeated the affirmation three times and then I went to the karate spot on the side of the hand and tapping lightly about 7 times, I repeated the affirmation 3 times, Rose was following me all the time.

Next we went through the remainder of the sequence with the shortened version of the affirmation, tapping on the head lightly about 7 times I would say, "This heart attack ruined my holiday", we repeated the affirmation three times and proceeded to tap on the other points lightly and repeated the affirmation. When we completed the sequence I asked Rose,

Me: How are you feeling now Rose?

Rose: Much calmer, I'm not so angry about my holiday being ruined now and my husband was really working too hard previously. He had been warned by his doctors to take things a little easier and I suppose he could have got his heart attack anywhere.

Me: Let's do another round of tapping and saying, "Even though I am not so angry and my husband could have had his heart attack anywhere else, I love and accept myself unconditionally."

We went through the whole process and I asked her how she felt?

Rose: Much better. I feel about a '1' and I feel calm about the holiday.

Me: I want to you repeat this after me (I was going to introduce the forgiving and letting go affirmations), "Even though I was angry for my holiday being ruined and my husband having a heart attack, I forgive myself for being angry and love and accept myself unconditionally." Repeat and follow what I am doing.

We did the tapping from the beginning with the sore spot and karate chop side of hand and did the rest of the tapping with the shortened version, which was just, "Holiday being ruined and I forgive myself." After this round of tapping and doing the whole sequence on the second round, I changed the affirmation to, "Even though my holiday was ruined by this incident, I forgive myself and I ask my cells to release the memories of the incident, and I love and accept myself unconditionally." We did one round and then I asked her how she felt.

Me: Rose, What is happening inside you now and how are you feeling?

Rose: I feel OK about the incident and I'm quite pleased that we were on holiday at the time when this happened to my husband because we both had a rest. (Now this is such a change from the other story that we began with)

I asked Rose to do another round of tapping, but this time I was going to introduce the gratitude process, I said to Rose to follow me again with the tapping and repeating the following affirmation. "Even though this happened, I am grateful that the worst didn't happen to my husband, he could have had a severe attack and perhaps died or been paralysed, but that didn't happen and he is recovering. I am grateful that we both also had a holiday and that he was cared for over there. I forgive myself for being so ungrateful, complaining about the money and he being ill, when I should be so grateful that nothing worse happened and that we have ample money anyway to be able to go away on holiday. I love and approve of myself even though I wasn't grateful." We did a round of tapping and the shortened version was just, ***"being ungrateful".***

Having done that round of tapping I asked her how she felt.

Me: Rose, how do you feel about the whole incident now?

Rose: Good, I feel so grateful that nothing worse happened to my husband and really silly about the money. We aren't wealthy, but comfortable and I'm shocked that I think that way.

Me: Do you still feel the same as when you came to see me?

Rose: No, I feel so good. I feel like a cloud has been lifted.

Me: Testing again: Rose, think again about your holiday and your husband having a heart attack, how do you feel about it?

Rose: I'm OK about it and I'm glad that my husband didn't get anything worse. I think it was his fault anyway for working so hard, but I'm glad that he's able to take it easy now.

Again, I have shown you that by asking questions you get the person to shift and understand more about the situations. I want you to ask yourself lots of questions when you are doing the breathing, tapping and affirmation and after each round test yourself.

This was the tip of the iceberg with Rose, we had many more sessions to deal with her other problems, but the main cause of all her problems was she had such high expectations for her life and of course, she was disappointed most of the time as her expectations weren't met. This is why she had such high and low swings throughout her life.

When she started off with her holiday, she had this vision of how the holiday would go and how she and her husband would enjoy the holiday, and of course it didn't happen that way. It was a total nightmare when he had his heart attack and not until we did the tapping and affirmations did she have a different perspective of 'what is'.

During the sessions that followed, she realised that her mother installed most of the patterns she had within her. Her mother had high expectations and was also very religious and when things didn't go according to plan, her mother would think that God was punishing her; of course Rose developed the same belief. When we did the tapping about God punishing her, she came out of it saying how stupid she felt and was able to release her mother's patterns that she had inherited. Now she is trying to be more in the present and accept 'what is', and is trying to be OK when things don't go her way. She knows that when things don't go her way now, it because of her expectations and she is learning how to let go of control. At least now she knows that it is not God that is punishing her.

I would stress that this book is not about you becoming a therapist and treating others.

This is a self-help book. If you stick to the basis of what I have introduced you to in the last two chapters, you will be able to contain your loss of life force. After all, ***this entire book is written to inform you about how to maintain your life force and become a good energy banker. When you run your energy correctly or are able to undo your blockages, you will have good health and visits to the doctor or taking medication will certainly be less, or a thing of the past. Key is for you to know yourself and to love yourself unconditionally.***

Practice Gratitude

"The real voyage of discovery consists not in seeking new landscapes but in having new eyes." Marcel Proust

I practise gratitude every morning and every evening and many times throughout the day. I will say to my Universe (to those of you who are religious 'God') first thing when my eyes are opened in the morning, "Thank you for allowing me to live another day. Thank you for my well being. Thank you for my food and shelter, thank you for what money I have to be able to live in this world. ***Finally, thank you for all the experiences that I am going to have today."***

In the evening when I am going to sleep I will say, "Thank you for all the experiences that I have had, even though some of the experiences didn't come up to my expectations, I have to learn to accept and live in the moment. Although I didn't embrace all of the experiences with an open heart today, I know that there are many lessons there for me to learn. Thank you for my food and the roof over my head and what money I have. Thank you for making sure that I am all right and providing me with abundance, even though I am not appreciative of it at times as I am so wrapped up in being a victim. Finally, thank you for reminding me who I am."

This last part is to remind me ***that I am a spiritual being only having human experiences***. When I ***do*** remember that I am a spiritual being, I recognise that I am perfect. This is easier said than done because there are so many distractions out in the external worlds to distract us from being in present time. This causes us to doubt who we really are. To be present and to know that we are spiritual beings takes lots of practice and faith. Being in the now and accepting 'what is' is the most difficult task because it all depends on trust and faith that everything is already all right, which is against all our programming.

Throughout the day I will say thank you to my universe for whatever situation that I am in. If something acceptable and beneficial happens, I will say thank you for it. If something doesn't meet my expectation and I find that difficult to accept because of my expectations and conditioning, I will still say thank you for this experience and I am grateful for the experience, even though I may not like what has happened. I will remind myself how blessed I am with abundance and all the good things that have happened in my life. ***I always remind myself that there are others who are in a less fortunate situation than me.*** I know there are billions of people who don't have the basics of life, or enough food, shelter or clean water, and millions that are ill with terminal diseases.

This reminds me how fortunate I am now.

When I compare myself to the majority of people in the world that have so very little, I realise that I am truly blessed in spite of what I have gone through in this moment. With this statement I breathe deeply, tap and soon become "very OK at NOT being OK".

It is so vital that we practise gratitude daily and in every moment that we can remember. Doing this keeps us OUT of the victim mode. Practising Gratitude reminds us of the abundance of 'what we have' rather than being in the lack of what we don't have. When we are blissful with what we have, we don't lose energy thinking about what we may not have or don't have.

BEING IN PRESENT TIME

Being in the NOW is one of the most difficult tasks. We have been programmed to compare all the time; we never stop judging. I am going to share with you a technique on how to be in present time. Before you begin, you have to be aware of your breathing patterns. When you can remember to breathe deeply for 4 or 5 seconds, or longer, with an in and out breath that is balanced, you will experience being in present time by breathing consciously. ***Breathing consciously puts you in the present moment and stops you losing your life force. Your mind is in the here and now, in the present, not thinking because your focus in on your breath. If you find it difficult to still your mind, just let the thoughts come and go, and keep your focus on breathing in and out, eventually your mind will be still.***

To put yourself in present time, place all your attention around your bellybutton area and breathe deeply into that area. You can either breathe in and out through your mouth or in and out through your nose. The count should be about 4-6 seconds in and 4-6 out. When you place all your attention on your breath, your mind actually starts to go blank as you concentrate on your breathing. There are no other distractions except the sound of your breath. When you do this for a few seconds, you are actually in the here and now and nowhere else. Your mind goes blank as you are not thinking or putting your opinions onto anything. You will then begin to understand what it is like to be a watcher and notice the new experiences that you are having.

When you are breathing in and out in long breaths, notice how different you feel inside, how much calmer you are getting and then begin to look around you and notice that you are just looking at whatever it is you are looking at. Whatever is there is there; you make no judgements of what you are looking at or listening to as you are only paying attention to the sound of your long breaths in your body. You will probably be able to hold this sensation for a few seconds and with constant practice, you will be able to do it for minutes at a time and then longer, having short breaks in between. ***Personally, I find that to remember to breathe long breaths is the most difficult part as I often forget to breathe deeply consciously***. When I am not breathing consciously my mind starts to wander.

When you are able to do this consistently, start to move your attention from your bellybutton area to your Heart Centre area (the heart centre is the area between your nipples in the middle of your chest). When you are in your Heart Centre, your breath will still be long and you will have new sensations. You will be able to hear your heart beat, and feel it. You will be totally within yourself and at one with yourself. Being in the Heart Centre is really the ultimate of being here and now. When you are in the Heart Centre you are able to feel love (to those of you that don't know what 'love' feels like, then you can resonate it to something like a calmness or peacefulness).

Being in this space you easily become more acceptable of 'what is'. The problem is, we shift in and out of our minds so quickly and we get so easily distracted with what is outside of us. When we pay attention to the outside, we lose the contact with the inside. To be proficient at this and to be acceptable of 'what is', you would have done hundred of hours of practice in the art of letting go of judgements, having no expectations and being aware of being in the now. You will probably then have a sense and understanding of some of the great teachings of the masters from the past.

In the early days, I practised being in the present whenever I could remember. It was very difficult to start off with as my monkey brain was always keeping me distracted with all sorts of thoughts and judgements. The deep breathing helped tremendously, ***when I remembered to do the breathing***. With constant observation and noticing of my patterns, I was able to remind myself more often throughout the day to breathe deeply consciously.

In the morning, when I am thanking my universe, I start to breathe deeply. When I visit the bathroom, I will remember to be present and breathing deeply when I first have my morning bodily functions. Then, I will carry on with this with my shaving and teeth brushing. Of course, when I first started this, I would forget to breathe deeply, but with constantly reminding myself, I would pull my attention back and start the deep breathing. ***In the early days, I would have sticky notes on the walls in the bathroom, kitchen and everywhere in the house reminding me to breathe deeply and be in the present.*** This forgetting to breathe deeply happens on and off during the day. When doing the breathing and being in present time, there seems to be such calmness around me and I don't seem to be in such a rush, as my day seems to flow so peacefully.

At breakfast and mealtimes, I again try to be 100% present. I try to chew my food a minimum of 25 times, of course, for some food this might be difficult. In instances like this, I chew for as long as there is food in my mouth before I take the next mouthful. Have you noticed how we stuff food into our mouth even before swallowing the last mouthful? When I am present with my food, I don't listen to the radio, watch the TV or read the newspapers. This allows me to be in great calmness and I really enjoy my meals more and don't have any digestion problems. Also, the food is actually much tastier when being in the present. If I need to talk, I will try to talk after I have finished the meal. Of course, this is difficult as others would think that I am rude, so yes, I do have conversations during mealtimes when I can't help it. This is why I prefer to eat alone or with people who understand what being present with food means.

I have now stopped listening to the radio in the car and just concentrate on my breathing deeply and being centred on my driving. There seems to be such stillness in my mind and the journey becomes timeless as I spend the time in the now. I will be calm even when there is a traffic jam or if someone cuts me up or honks at me; it doesn't bother me one little bit. I have learnt that being in the now, I am the watcher and accept what is around me. I am not caught up in other people's madness or impatience and watch the day unfold. I have learnt that being stressed out will not make the traffic move faster, or make someone drive better. I have learnt that being late is also all right as I can't do anything about the traffic jams. These situations are out of my control and I don't have to lose energy about it now that I know this.

When I am travelling by public transport, I will try to be totally present when I remember doing my deep breathing consciously, and if I happen to be reading a book on the train, I will be reading and doing my breathing, this keeps me present and totally in the now with what I am doing. And if I am not reading, I will just breathe deeply and just watch what is happening around me with no judgements. The time just passes by and before I know it I will be at my destination totally calm and energised.

When I am at the Supermarket queuing to check out, I will be totally present at the till and doing my breathing deeply and observing. Previously, I would be judging the till girls or customers before me, looking into their trolleys observing and judging what they are buying and being impatient at the same time while waiting to be checked out. Not anymore, what is the point of wasting my valuable life force on such small matters?

The above are some of the practices that I perform in my typical days and I try to be present most of the time. Of course, I am not able to maintain this stance all the time. ***I have periods where I also lose it and go into judgements and start to lose energy, but I can now, very quickly, bring myself back into present time by remembering to do my conscious breathing and the process***. I have found with practice that I don't have to use the process as often as I used to because the conscious breathing alone keeps me in the present. If I lose my cool, I can quickly start the process and within seconds I am OK and acceptable with 'what is'. There are still some biggies that I encounter from time to time that keep me in judgements and cause me to lose energy, but each day that passes by when I am being tested, it gets easier each time.

The above technique has helped hundreds of others, as well as myself with balancing our energies and being in present time. I strongly suggest that you try it and find out for yourself how it may assist you in your daily lives. Remember that if you don't put the effort in, nothing will happen and you will just be the same old you. ***You are***

the product of all your past experiences and if you are not happy with who you are, then all you have to do is take the first step to change.

Remodelling You To Go Forward

"Love, and do what you like." St. Augustine

Remember in my earlier chapters I mentioned that you are similar to a computer and that you have been programmed by your guardians and your early learning environments to become the person you are today. You are probably not entirely content with the current model of you and I am in no doubt that there are certain characteristics of yourself that you find objectionable. In order for you to know your weaknesses and strengths consciously, I would recommend that you make a list of them so that you can refer to it often to address the characteristics that you are not contented with.

I would like you to begin with your strengths first and then we will work with your weaknesses. Please record ***all the qualities that you like about yourself***. What you are good at, what qualities you possess etc. Take your time and go through your whole life and try remembering all the good deeds you have done and enjoyed. Who did you help? What hobbies do you have? What sports were you good at school? What were your favourite subjects at school and which ones did you excel in? These are some categories for you to start with. I am sure you will be able to add more to the list as you begin with your list. If necessary, talk to a close friend and ask them what they see as your strengths.

Next, list all the weaknesses in your character. What is it that you dislike about yourself? When you have finished your list, I want you to go through your list and ask yourself some questions.

Let's say your list looks like this: (Obviously there are going to be many things that you will be listing. This is only an example of how it may appear).

1. I am lazy
2. I never finish the task that I start
3. I am untidy
4. I am useless at sports
5. Nobody loves me
6. I am not able to meet people
7. I am rubbish at everything that I do

And the list goes on etc............

Now use this format with each item on your list.

1. "I am lazy."

Ask yourself: "If I am lazy, who told me this?"

(A possible answer: *" Probably my mum, she was always nagging me.")*

Ask yourself: "What is the evidence to prove that I am lazy?"

(A possible answer*: "My room is always untidy and I am an untidy person.")*

This exercise is going to take some time for you to complete for all your weaknesses. When you have completed this exercise, you will see a pattern, often it is your parents or caretakers who installed most of your weakness. This is not to say it is a good or bad thing, it is just how things are. You just believed and accepted their beliefs and didn't bother to challenge them because you didn't know any better. You placed your trust in them and accepted that their words were the truth. However, you don't have to keep these beliefs now if you are dissatisfied with your current situation. You can delete, like any computer programme and put in a new programme/belief. How do you do this? You go through the breathing and tapping process together, as explained in earlier chapters.

Here is the affirmation for changing belief.
"Even though ***I am lazy***, and that is ***what my mum told me consistently when I was young, and my room is untidy,*** I am willing to accept myself unconditionally".

When you are comfortable at accepting yourself by using the tapping and breathing techniques, you may change the wording to, "Even though.............. ***I love and approve of myself unconditionally,"*** With each weakness, take an intensity count and work with it until the intensity of the feelings comes down to zero.

Then, go through the remaining procedures as described in the breathing and tapping chapters. As you complete each weakness retest your weakness and ask yourself how you feel about yourself now. You should be feeling better each time you have completed each weakness with the process. ***If you don't feel any different, go back and repeat the process again from the beginning.***

Your list of your strengths is for you to look at periodically to remind yourself of your strengths. It is important for you to better familiarise yourself to impose your positive beliefs in your programming as we have in the past, on a daily basis judged, ourselves negatively. When you have acquired new behaviour patterns that become your strength, you can add this to your list and in time, you will see that you have acquired new beliefs and have changed.

THE FUTURE WILL DEFINITELY POSITIVELY CHANGE

When you have remodelled yourself on a daily basis, you will discover that your outlook on life will be very different. You will definitely ***do different things from your past*** and most importantly you will have loved yourself and now have high self-esteem. You will not need approval of others, you will not worry or care what others think as you have learnt that everybody, from their point of view, is right but that is not the truth, it is only their truth. You will learn to respect others' opinions and allow others to be who they are. Judgement will be a thing of the past as you have learnt to love and accept yourself unconditionally.

You will wear what you feel comfortable with and not dress up in some designer gear because it is the 'in' thing to wear; you will do what feels right for you and not for others. Others will consider you to be selfish and arrogant because you will do what you feel is right and not out of obligation. In short, so much will change that others will not like the changed you. They will be scared by the change in you. Some people will want you to be dependent on them. Others will be jealous.

The journey will then seem to be difficult as you are learning to love your own company more, but the good news is, the more you are learning to appreciate your own company you will make contact with your inner self, the real you. This space represents different situations to different people. I will let you find out what it is for yourself. For me, when I am in that deep space of my inner self I feel total love, I am not afraid, I know that everything is OK, and that I am loved and being protected by my universe. I have a sense that I am already perfect. Everything is just perfect inside me and I am totally calm and relaxed. My day just past by with me just being the watcher of what is going on around me. I am just the observer of life and watch everyone go about their business without any judgement. I know within myself that all is perfect as it is.

Of course, it is not like this all the time as I do lose it, and that is when I have to keep reminding myself to be in the present and reminding myself that I am a spiritual being having human experiences.

In hindsight I will say that the daily journey has now become easier after a very resisting start as I was resistant to change. I would say that I am more accepting of situations around me today and I have my energy in balance most of the time. I know I am healthier now at the age of 63 than when I was younger and I am more relaxed about life and very acceptable of what life is around me.

I know that if you do the exercises that I have shared with you in the earlier chapters and re-read this book several times to understand you are an energetic being and have been programmed, ***you will definitely change***. If you only just read this particular chapter a few times, your life will be different. You will learn how to be a good energetic banker and your outlook on life will be different. You will look with new eyes. When you are feeling low, depressed, impatient or lost and for each of your worries, just remember that you have choices.

You can EITHER not accept "what is" and not be OK about it and repeat your judgements, old behavioural patterns and deplete your life force and become eventually ill, OR you can choose to be acceptable of "what is" and being OK with NOT being OK sustaining your life force and having a healthy life.

I know in my heart which route you will take. I praise you for taking the courage to change yourself and begin to love yourself a little more each day. Eventually, you will remember and know who you are and love yourself unconditionally. I know, as from today your life will change. You have the choice now.

I wish you good health, fun and an abundance of experiences in the near future knowing that you will be, "OK NOT being OK" with it.

You can reach me at arramkong@aol.com if you need any clarification about your situation. I promise to reply to you and give you support wherever possible.

Finally, here are some very simple rules to abide by daily.

- ***Make no judgements (every judgement made, causes one to lose energy)***
- ***Everybody is right from their opinion, but it is not the truth, therefore allow everyone to be who they want to be.***
- ***Have no expectations. Accept everything and nothing at the same time, this way you will always be surprised.***
- ***Give up the need to know "why things happen as they do."***
- ***Trust that the unscheduled events in your lives are a form of spiritual direction.***
- ***Have the courage to make the choices you need to make, accept what you cannot change and have the wisdom to know the difference.***
- ***Resistance creates a barrier. Acceptance dissolves it. Unless one accepts what has happened without resistance, one will never find the answer one seeks.***
- ***Unless you are happy NOW, you will never find happiness. So if you are not happy now, stop trying to find happiness in the future and bring your attention to the present moment. That is where your happiness is.***
- ***Practise gratitude daily.***

About The Author

Arram Kong (Dip L.S.I. EFT-ADV) is an Energy Healer and teacher with over 25 years experience in self-development work. He is a highly developed healer, and uses dynamic higher dimensional healing techniques, including sound, crystal and accelerated Reiki Master's techniques.

Arram is a Reiki Master, certified teacher of the Louise Hay Philosophy "You Can Heal Your Life", a NLP practitioner (The Art and Science of Human Excellence), therapist and metaphysical counselor. He is a graduate from the London School of Iridology and a Certified Taoist Practitioner. He has been through intensive training with a leading Taoist Master who has handed down his most sacred and closely held Taoist practices, formulas and methods of internal alchemy. He is also a certified practitioner of Reconnective Healing and Meridian Therapies.

Arram conducts private sessions and group workshops in London coaching the contents of "It's Ok NOT to be OK". If you would like further details or host a workshop in your area please contact him or visit his website at www.arramkong.co.uk.

For questions or comments about this book, please e-mail:

arramkong@aol.com

Copies of this book can be obtained direct from the publisher in the UK at the address shown below priced at £11.99 each plus £2.01 postage & packing per book for UK. Total £14.00

(Overseas add £4.01 postage & packing per book for airmail).

Total £16.00

Please make cheques Payable to A.Kong.

Or you may order direct from website with your Credit Card:
www.arramkong.co.uk

Publications are also available at quantity discounts with bulk purchases.

Published by A Kong Publishing

2 Corringham Road, Wembley Park. Middlesex . HA9 9QA
England.